Voice Of Nature
My Life & Daily Chronicles
(Vol.1)

Sandra Duru

VOICE OF NATURE: My Life & Daily Chronicles (Vol 1) by Sandra Duru

Published by Mgbeke Media Publishing

Visit the author's website at www.mgbeke.media
Copyright © 2022 by Sandra Duru

All rights reserved. No portion of this book may be reproduced in any form without permission from the author, except as permitted by U.S. copyright laws. To ask for permission, contact: info@mgbeke.media

Cover by Empress Creations

ISBN

979-8-9865706-3-1

Printed in the United States of America
First Edition

Disclaimer: The author assures that, as much as many direct references are made to The Bible and Christian faith in these unique quotes, this is in no way an attempt to coerce, force it on, or unsettle anyone or any other religion. Inspiration is everywhere around us in nature, and it thrives when there is a spiritual connection that the author deeply enjoys, hence the frequent references. The author assumes no liability for allegations of harm therefrom, and also assumes no liability for action taken because of the information herein.

ACKNOWLEDGEMENT

To the King of Kings, Lord of Lords, and Creator of all things, who has more than shown and proven through my life that "impossible" is nothing indeed!

In the fiercest opposition and unforeseen challenges, HE stood firmly by me and mine, ensuring we had come through unscathed.

To HIM, whose blessings and wisdom continually well up in me and have become a limitless spring of destiny-changing and impactful ideas and projects to help shape countless lives to be more and do more in life.

To my late father, Sir Benedict C. Duru: Your words of wisdom, lessons, and instructions have helped your small "Mgbeke" daughter become an accomplished, renowned, and widely respected lady of class, substance, and immeasurable value. If I could come to this world again, I would still choose you as my father and hope to get much more time with you than I did in this one. I love you always, Papa.

As always, my most profound appreciation goes to my "Three Musketeers" - Anita, Igwe, and Dikesinachi. You are more than just my children. You are everything to me, and even more. Thank you all for always being my support system, cheerleaders, shoulders to lean and cry on in need, gist and play partners, greatest motivation and inspiration, and above all, the reason why failure has never and can never exist in my world! I love you guys to the moon and back. Always and forever!

AUTHOR'S BIO

Dr. Sandra C. Duru is a street-smart spiritual warrior whose knowledge-of-self game is extra tight. The CEO of MGBEKE LLC, TUFF INCORPORATED, and WENETLY has weathered massive storms of life and had her eyes opened and her heart broken severely many times. However, her mental toughness and strength have remained unshakable through it all.

If anyone could make being broken look beautiful, it is her. Her strength keeps her going, and she believes in every inch of this universe. She loves life with all her heart, and it loves her right back. Hence, she's always been essential in other people's lives.

Dr. Duru is a Life Coach, Successful Business Woman, Entrepreneur, Media & Public Relations Consultant, Education Consultant, Psychologist, Information Strategist, Herbal Medicine Practitioner, and Motivational Speaker. She is also an astutely Creative Writer, Talent Discovery, Development & Management Consultant, and an Infinite Solution Provider to general life issues.

She also doubles as a Certified Career Counselor, Certified Democratic Leadership Trainer, Certified Lobbyist & Negotiator, and Life & Business Strategist.

Dr. Duru is a lover and a protector; she's courageous and incredibly strong. She has faced more struggles than other people can ever imagine. Having been rejected and disowned at age 15, she grew up without any relatives or family. Her life's journey has been a combination of Joseph's and Job's stories. She's also endured a harrowing experience that could be likened to Potiphar's wife's malicious accusations when she was falsely accused of trafficking her children into the United States of America.

As Managing Director, CEO, and owner of Sanchhy Nigeria Limited, Zest Media & Entertainment, and Excellence Cables & Electronics Company,

Dr. Duru temporarily lost all these enormous corporations and many more within a very short time in 2016. She had to start from scratch in a faraway country with her three children and no one to support or help but God.

Such has been her very Joseph-and-Job-like experiences in life, but like them, God has been gracious to her all through. Today, she stands in joyous celebrations and victory over all her past afflictions, and she does so with a massive bag of inspirational stories and experiences to share in her daily Soul Tonics.

She is aware that she has no limits. Her growth game is on fleek, and her boundaries keep her in check. This is why she lives in the present moment but has a big vision for her future. She surely knows what it means to have been branded a "big failure," having hit severe rock bottoms in business and her personal life.

Now, Dr. Duru walks around with the moon in her heart and the stars in her eyes. She lives in the deep, and her patience is eternal. She has passed through the furnace, and her scars tell the story. Having dined with the devil, she now rides on the back of angels. She is her storm and the hero of her story.

Fondly known as the "Undefeated Village Girl," she speaks in parables and listens with compassion. She feels every energy and understands every vibration. This is why her patience is eternal, and her love is her superpower.

.

INTRODUCTION

Another blessed and beautiful year is upon us, and it is a pleasure and honor for me to share this year with you.

I'm sure you must have made many new resolutions again this year, but how have you kept to any of those resolutions in the past years? Don't get me wrong; making resolutions is excellent, but keeping and staying true to them is way better.

Voice of Nature - My Life & Daily Chronicles is designed to help you accomplish several significant goals this year. Still, the most essential aim of this project is to draw your attention inwards first of all, before you now relaunch yourself at your objectives daily this year.

The voice of nature is within and all around you, and if you listen deep and well enough, you will be amazed at how much motivation, inspiration, drive, and power you've always had within you to pursue, overtake, and conquer all your dreams!

These voices are the soft, still thoughts, nuggets, and ideas that come, and you roll them around in your mind as you awake and throughout the day many times, but rarely act on any of them.

Hence, this book offers daily motivational and wisdom nuggets designed to inspire and provoke readers to be more direct and intentional about their daily lives.

While helping them develop mental toughness as they apply the daily nuggets, it is also designed to help any seemingly average person with no recognized writing skills develop a passion for it by documenting their daily activities while also grooming several top writers among them, too, in the process.

If my life's journey and story could inspire a best-selling motivational and inspirational book and materials that have and are still blessing millions of people worldwide, I see no reason why a passionate chronicle of your life cannot be subsequently compiled into a highly inspiring and successful material, too.

As you are determined that this year is much better than your previous years, please take the necessary action to ensure it turns out that way by taking calculated and deliberate steps toward your goals.

And, what better way to do that than for you to begin each day with these unique voices of nature wisdom nuggets, apply them to your activities, and then record each day's challenges, obstacles, and subsequent victories as your life and daily chronicles.

I look forward to seeing you at the top...this new year and always.

Do remain richly blessed.

DEDICATION

To The ONE who sits enthroned over all wisdom, knowledge, inventions, crafts, ideas, and wit in everything created. After all, by HIM were all things made, and there is nothing made that was made without HIM!

To my "Three Musketeers" - Anita, Igwe, and Dikesinachi - if there is a life after this one, I would love to have you all in my life again. "Amazing" does not even scratch the surface of what you are to me. This one is for you guys. I love you!

CONTENT

QUARTER 1:   Day 1 to Day 90   Page 1 - Page 90

QUARTERLY SELF-APPRAISAL | REVIEW

QUARTER 2:   Day 91 to Day 181   Page 92 - Page 182

QUARTERLY SELF-APPRAISAL | REVIEW

QUARTER 3:   Day 182 to Day 273   Page 184 - Page 275

QUARTERLY SELF-APPRAISAL | REVIEW

QUARTER 4:   Day 274 to Day 365   Page 277 - Page 368

QUARTERLY SELF-APPRAISAL | REVIEW

CONCLUSION | YEAR-END AUDIT   Page 369 - Page 370

SYNOPSIS   Page 373

QUARTER 1:

DAY 1 - DAY 90

Voice Of Nature (Vol.1) By Sandra Duru

Day 1

"Stop trying to answer or explain yourself to anyone. Let God finish with you. Keep going, and one day your life will speak for itself, and all eyes shall see." - Dr. Sandra C. Duru

There's No Better Spokesperson You Can Have But God - Keep Going!

My beloved friend, if there is one thing you must make up your mind never to do this New Year, it is to live your life based on any human validation or be desperate for gratification from anyone.

Keep your eyes on your Maker, and let all your hope and trust be in HIM alone. God will never bless you until HE has rid you of every impurity that can destroy HIS blessings in your life.

So, let HIM finish with you. Don't be in a hurry. Only keep pushing on and never relent; one day, all eyes shall see and glorify HIM, even as they celebrate you too!

How does this resonate with you, and how do you intend to use this voice of nature today?

Day 2

"Never compromise on your values, and do not be afraid of your oppressor. You are on a journey to fulfill destiny, so some people are desperate to see you fail." - Dr. Sandra C. Duru

A Life Of Compromise Shortchanges You - Resist It!

Hello today, my dear friend. Do you know that compromising your faith, values, principles, and ideals in life because of external pressure is relatively equal to picking up a gun and shooting yourself in the head?

Yes, it is equivalent to ending your life with your own hands, and you must never allow anyone to push you into such a terrible spot, no matter who they are! You are like a ship laden with the rarest and most precious jewels, so it is only natural for pirates and bandits to attack you.

Have you been experiencing these kinds of attacks repeatedly lately? Would you like to share your experiences with others so they can learn and be blessed, too?

Day 3

"Sometimes, God has to strip you of everything to get you to focus on the direction HE wants for your life." - Dr. Sandra C. Duru

Can You Ever Lose When You Depend On And Follow God Totally?

My love, do you know that God has a way of preparing us for the tasks, purpose, and plans HE had set for our lives even before we were formed in our mothers' wombs?

Hence, you can never lose anything or be defeated if you stand with HIM and follow diligently through faith. This is HIS word and promises to you; HE can never fail!

That trial and rough patch you're experiencing today may be HIS way of redirecting you back to HIMSELF. Hold on, don't fret, and everything will be fine sooner than you can imagine, my dear.

Day 4

"Your mind is your powerhouse. Once you lose that, you can never find a way out of any dire situation. So, protect and maintain your mental toughness always." - Dr. Sandra C. Duru

Your Mind Is More Than Mere Feelings - It Is Vital!

My dear friend, I trust that you are well and everything is great at your end today.

Have you ever been told that your mind is more than just a tool that forms, processes, and distributes your thoughts and will, but the most vital key to your achievements in life?

Yes, it is! Hence, even the good book says to "guard your heart with all diligence, for out of it are the issues of life." A healthy mind is a healthy and wealthy life, my dear. Anything less than this is an invitation for the enemy to prey on and destroy you, and you do not want that for yourself, now, do you?

Day 5

"The best houses are yet to be built, and the best jewelry pieces have not been made yet. Don't ever lose yourself in pursuing such fleeting and vain things in life." - Dr. Sandra C. Duru

Resist The Pursuit Of Vanity - It Never Yields Good!

A person's needs are always insatiable - once one is sorted, another seems to pop out, demanding to be taken care of, too. How, then, should we live our lives?

Never be weighed down or bothered by what you don't have today. The best is yet to come, and even those, too, shall pass away!

Day 6

"Your purpose is to be yourself. The full spectrum of your weirdness is what the world is waiting for. Return to your infant innocence!" – Dr. Sandra C. Duru

You Are Glorious, Not Incompetent - Be Yourself!

Have you ever stopped to think about why you seem to get so much hate, bitterness, envy, needless and unprovoked attacks, and destructive criticism laced with venomous jealousy on almost everything you lay your hands upon to do?

Have you ever wondered why the enemy tries to make you look and feel incompetent? The answer to this is straightforward, and I will share it with you in these few words today, as always. You are consistently under these attacks because of the extreme value you carry and your unique greatness.

Please don't let anything rob you of that purity and divine uniqueness, as these are the tools that shall unlock your glorious manifestation the world has awaited for so long! Continue being yourself, and never allow anything to change you for no reason. You will achieve your dreams and purpose in life.

Voice Of Nature (Vol.1) By Sandra Duru

Day 7

"If you run into a wall, don't ever turn around and give up just like that. Instead, you should always figure out how to climb it, go through it, walk around it, or even break right through it!" - Dr. Sandra C. Duru

Obstacles & Battles Are There To Be Conquered - Not To Subdue You!

I took a while to study the course of every river I've come across in life and compared it to that of the seas and oceans, and it left a massive impact on how I live my life and purpose.

No river has a straight course because it keeps bending at every sight of an obstacle. Seas and oceans, though, have countless mountains, cities, and even civilizations buried under them! Do you want to know why?

It's because an ocean never bends or retreats before an obstacle but runs through or over it. To become all you have been destined and created to be in life, you must stop acting like a river and, like the seas and oceans, confront and subdue all challenges before you. Yes, you can and will if you believe and stand firm in your faith!

Day 8

"Never let any adversary drag you down in life. Fight back and never break down in front of those standing against you. And, always stay focused on your journey and goals in life - never allow your trials to overwhelm you!" - Dr. Sandra C. Duru

Breaking Down Never Helps - Stand And Fight!

Do you know we are up against an enemy with zero mercy and empathy and one whose conscience has already been seared with a hot iron?

Instead of inspiring remorse or pity for you, your tears fuel his sadistic pleasure. Hence, you must never break and stay down weeping, no matter what this life throws at you!

Day 9

"Do not pray for your enemies to die. They are the vessels God used to push you into your destiny and place of rest. Don't wish them evil, and never see anyone as your enemy either." - Dr. Sandra C. Duru

No One Is Your Enemy In Life - They're Only Tools!

The words of King David in Psalm 23:5 always give me renewed hope and joy whenever I see the enemy move against me in anything I am trying to accomplish.

He said: "Thou preparest a table before me in the presence of mine enemies: Thou anointest my head with oil; my cup runneth over." God keeps those enemies alive and around you so that the glory HE brings your way may be even sweeter!

Day 10

"Always remember that the journey of your life is a process for purpose, and you must scale through any obstacle to get there." - Dr. Sandra C. Duru

The Only Thing Between You And Your Fulfilment Is That Obstacle - Crush It!

I can almost bet you've already heard that everything that happens to you in life is a process and phases designed to get you to a predetermined and predestinated purpose, right?

Well, what if I told you today that nothing will matter or amount to anything tangible if you do not stop being so timid and fearful because of all the opposition, afflictions, obstacles, and battles you face? Those obstacles were placed in your path to help make your story even more glorious. They must bow to you and not the other way around!

Day 11

"Iron sharpens iron, and you can only be as effective as your knowledge base. Hence, you must watch the company you keep because no relationship ever leaves you the same way!" - Dr. Sandra C. Duru

Ignorance Is A Deadlier Killer Than An Atomic Bomb - Flee From It!

One of the biggest lies ever told in the history of humanity is deeply embedded in that phrase many people use jokingly in most situations. They say: "What you don't know won't kill you," but I disagree with this notion in every context.

Yes, what you do not know can and will destroy, shortchange, limit, and eventually kill you if you keep yourself ignorant!

Day 12

"Success cannot be so tagged without the presence of seeming failure that you overcame. Stop sulking but pick yourself up whenever you fall - you are not a failure!" - Dr. Sandra C. Duru

Nothing Can Place A Tag On You If You Don't Accept It - You Are Not A Failure!

Do you know that you can never be tagged anything in this life if you've not accepted to be known and referred to as that thing?

And this refusal or refusal is not with words and arguments but with your determined, purposeful, and deliberate actions!

So, what should you do instead of crying and feeling down whenever the world places a label contrary to your destiny, and how should you react? With boldness, mental toughness, faith, and relentless courage because, God can never fail you! Refuse their evil labels and tags, my dear, and you will flourish.

Day 13

"As a born-achiever and someone destined to break out of obscurity by achieving greatness, you must start to see humiliations, pains, disappointments, and rejections as a redirection to your greatness!" - Dr. Sandra C. Duru

Pain Is A Redirection - It Doesn't Signify Rejection!

There is one thing synonymous with greatness, and it is always a part of the lives of people of great purpose and destinies in life - pain!

Are the constant encounters and experiences you see always laced with much pain? Do not worry or fret. This doesn't mean you're cursed or rejected at all.

Day 14

"You must start seeing every setback as an opportunity to achieve even greater heights than what you were reaching for before. This is what champions are made of!" - Dr. Sandra C. Duru

Adversity And Setbacks Are What Makes You A Champion - Embrace Them!

One of my favorite lines from the movie "Pompei" was something the gladiators brought into the coliseum to fight to the death would say before the fights began: "We that are about to die - We salute you!"

More often than not, the ones who survived embraced that present adversity, for what kills many in life is the fear of what is coming against them before it even comes! I learned a great lesson from this, and it has always been one of my mantras as I go through each day's setbacks, trials, obstacles, and whatever else comes my way.

Day 15

"Life will be what you see it as and what you make it to be. Hence, you must learn to see humiliations, disappointments, and rejections as a redirection to your greatness, and everything will always work out for you as you keep fighting on!" - Dr. Sandra C. Duru

Life is Easy - What You See Is What You Get!

One of my all-time favorite Bible stories describes what happened when God promised to make Abram the father of all nations before changing his name to Abraham.

God told him that HE would give him everything "as far as his eyes could see," and that promise is in effect to date. What does your life look like today? What do you see of yourself with your mind's eyes, and what do you speak into your life daily?

Day 16

"Pain is a sign that you are still alive. The fact that you feel pain could be a good thing, depending on how you view and use it. Turn your pain into power by refusing to let it bury you, and watch yourself smash your goals easily every day!" - Dr. Sandra C. Duru

Pain Is An Ally, Not Your Enemy - Use It!

There is a famous saying that many soldiers who have been to battle are conversant with: "It is only the living that hears the sounds of gunshots and feels pain." This profound truth applies to so many other things in our lives.

That pain is so unbearable and uncomfortable, yes, but do you realize that it's also an indication that you're still alive and can still overcome all these battles and obstacles if you don't relent?

Day 17

"Whatever hurdles life throws at you, keep moving forward, and pay no attention to distractions!" - Dr. Sandra C. Duru

Hurdles Can Either Motivate Or Distract You - Choose Wisely!

The day every human being alive was created, the scriptures say that God looked upon us and said that we "are good." In essence, this means more than we have opened our minds to.

Affirming that everything about you is good implies that the Creator confirmed that you're invaluable and placed no lid or limits on you.

So, today, I'd like to ask you again: Are these hurdles and challenges before you distractions or motivations? What you see is what you get, remember?

Day 18

"The destination matters, not what you go through on the journey. Keep your eyes on that, and ignore every other thing along the way." - Dr. Sandra C. Duru

All That Matters Is Your Destination - Keep Your Eyes On That Alone!

Countless challenges, battles, and obstacles will naturally spring up in your path as you forge ahead in your quest for greatness. You must often do some pretty hard and sometimes even imaginable things to survive.

Never let these situations dissuade, discourage, or break you and your desire to achieve your purpose in life. The end justifies the means, and all you need to do is stay focused on your destination - greatness, limitless opportunities, goodness, wealth, fulfillment, and glory!

Day 19

"There's a reason for your existence, so don't ever compromise your values for mere mortals. Keep whatever makes you who you are, and embrace your uniqueness without apologies!" - Dr. Sandra C. Duru

You Are Unique. You Are You - Never Apologize For It!

Many individuals have some uncanny resemblance in a lot of things about themselves. However, one mystery even science finds fascinating to date is that no two individuals are ever the same, no matter their similarities.

You were not made a copy of anything or anyone else but your Creator, and HE has also sealed your destiny and glory in its uniqueness. Find your purpose in life, give yourself to it wholly, excel at it, and never bother yourself about anything or anyone else...ever!

Day 20

"The truth is that no one owes you anything in life! Allowing bitterness to grow in your heart against anyone will only rob and limit you in life."
- Dr. Sandra C. Duru

Bitterness Is Corrosive - It Destroys Both Ways!

One severe threat to the health of anyone who gets involved in holding grudges and being bitter against others is the threat of being consumed by the hate and venom they bottle within!

Nothing good can ever come from allowing such darkness to fester inside you, and you must rid yourself of such against anyone, no matter what they may have done or are doing against you. It is for your good.

Day 21

"Don't ever blame anybody for your failure or success. You are in this life by yourself, and you must make it work for you, no matter the odds you face!" - Dr. Sandra C. Duru

Nobody Is Ever To Blame For Your Life's Outcomes - You Are In Charge!

One of the most damaging mistakes I have seen many young people make these days is to keep trying to pass the buck of the blame for their current situation to every other person but themselves.

Yes, your parents were poor and couldn't afford to give you a quality education and life. Yes, your father was a deadbeat and never around. However, where these situations lead you in life is entirely your responsibility and fault if things end negatively for you - not theirs!

Day 22

"When you have a dream, no one can understand it like you do because it is yours. The fastest way to kill yourself and your vision is to start sharing or discussing it prematurely!" - Dr. Sandra C. Duru

Your Dream Is Your Child - Don't Push Out Prematurely!

The term: "pregnant with ideas" is a profound one that many people use idly, yet many do not understand how deep and significant it is to our lives.

Your dreams, visions, goals, purpose, and calling in life are like a child in the womb, and you must carefully nurture, guard, and protect it. Sharing too early is like over-exposing pregnancy at a delicate stage, and also like trying to push out a baby before the due date.

Day 23

"If you must accomplish all you want to do and become, sometimes you must be lonely. Don't get discouraged and allow your courage and determination to drop because you find yourself isolated while pursuing your dreams." - Dr. Sandra C. Duru

The Path To Greatness Is Not Crowded - Don't Be Discouraged!

Are you on a quest to achieve a uniquely great thing, or are you pursuing a goal that you know is right yet seems contrary to public opinion and stand? Never let that deter or bother you!

Remember that even our Lord Jesus says, "narrow is the way that leads to life, and they be few that find it." Don't let the fact that it seems you're alone on your path now bother you. You're on the right track, and you will excel.

Day 24

"Don't be afraid of being alone as you build. You are on a path to greatness, and in due time, the world will celebrate you too."
- Dr. Sandra C. Duru

Don't Mind The Lonely Path - Greatness Awaits Ahead!

Man was created as a social creature that makes us all crave companionship occasionally. This is perfectly understandable.

However, you must know and understand that the path that leads to unique greatness in life is never crowded and mostly very lonely. Keep forging ahead even if you're standing alone now. It will all make sense and yield tremendous rewards soon.

Day 25

"Never hang around people fond of judging others or gossiping about others. No one on a path and journey to greatness meddles with such things!" - Dr. Sandra C. Duru

Gossip Is Self-Sabotage - Never Engage In It!

Do you know that an athlete running in a sprint race never has time to look at the others running alongside them?

Such loss of focus and triviality will prove very costly for the athlete in that race, and no serious one engages in such. This is the same with you and how you should pursue your dreams, visions, goals, and purpose in life.

There is an unspoken rule that everyone who has and those who also intend to achieve greatness in this life must follow, and it is clearly stated in the voice of nature's quote for you today.

Day 26

"Ease and comfort have always been the enemies of growth and development, whether as individuals or corporate entities. Hence, you must fight to keep aiming higher anytime you're in a spot that's getting too comfortable for you!" - Dr. Sandra C. Duru

Too Much Ease Is An Enemy - Avoid It!

If there's one thing I am very confident of in this life, we all want to live comfortably and in as much luxury as we can afford.

However, what if I told you that this quest for comfort might become your undoing and the reason you may miss out on your God-given purpose in life if the utmost care is not taken?

Anything you find so much ease and almost no difficulty getting done is on a pedestal that you have significantly grown and evolved beyond. Move on!

Day 27

"Do you know that what has broken and killed many has also fueled countless dreams? You can turn that mockery into strength and power and a ladder to take you to your expected destination to fulfill your destiny!" - Dr. Sandra C. Duru

Turn That Mockery Into Strength - Don't Let It Bury You!

Are you aware that the same things that have sent some people to the grave have also lifted many others to worldwide acclaim and prominence?

Some people become a shell of themselves, withdraw, slide into depression, and eventually take their own lives when subjected to significant abuse, mockery, unprovoked malicious attacks, and such evils.

However, others like me use these setbacks as manure to grow; hence, instead of stumbling blocks, they become stepping stones to my purpose and goals. You can do the same too!

Day 28

"It doesn't matter what you've been called because you are your authentic self and refuse to compromise your values and standards. Keep being on the right track, and never let it bother you. It may take some time, but you will never regret your actions." - Dr. Sandra C. Duru

Stay On Course, No Matter The Taunts - It Will Pay Off!

One of the funniest things I've observed both personally and in history is the fact that many who tease, malign, call you names, try to bully, and taunt you while in pursuit of your God-given purpose are also the same ones who are quick to shout your praise and celebrate you when you achieve greatness.

What is the moral for you today? Never let their sinister jeers and malicious slander get to you! Do all you can to ensure that you stay on course, and very soon, they shall wipe the floor before you with the same mouths they used to mock you.

Day 29

"Let your success speak for you. The only way to achieve this is to remain focused, pay no attention to distractions, and ignore your mockers." - Dr. Sandra C. Duru

Your Works Speak Louder Than Your Voice Ever Will - Put In Your All!

There's a saying I've always loved, not only because it is so true but because I keep seeing the genuineness of wisdom in almost everything I do and all around me.

It is said that every man's work is a selection of who he is, and even the scriptures say that by their fruits, we shall know them.

So, if you ever want to make the best impression in life, ensure that the things you do and how you do them are excellent and that you're wholly focused on consistently delivering premium quality! This way, you will not need to reply to your detractors and enemies along your path.

Day 30

"The journey to true greatness and self-actualization in life is not a sprint but a marathon. It has different paths, phases, and many experiences and emotions." - Dr. Sandra C. Duru

Success Is A Journey Filled With Many Paths & Phases - Hang On!

Many people have described some great persons as "overnight successes," and that term never fails to crack me up. Why? There is no such thing!

Real success, true greatness, and fulfillment in life are not something you can stumble on or fluke. It is a journey filled with consistent, deliberate, and well-calculated steps with the end in focus.

Never let anyone pressure, deceive, or make you feel like you're a failure or inadequate because you're not "blowing" overnight.

Day 31

"Nothing good in this life ever comes easy. You must brace yourself for today's severe pains to enjoy tomorrow's sweet gains." - Dr. Sandra C. Duru

Today's Pains Are Tomorrow's Gains - Brace Up!

Many people today make the mistake of thinking and expecting good things to come or happen for them without any suffering or pain. However, the sad but honest reality is that this will never be!

Even our Lord says, "Except a grain of corn first falls to the ground and dies, it abides alone." You can never achieve that level of greatness, fruitfulness, and productivity without going through the painful process that will prepare and help you birth them.

Day 32

"The fact that man not only flies now but has even broken never before imagined limits in these "flying contraptions" proves that victory is only for those who dare to fight and not hide in fear. What do you choose to do today?" - Dr. Sandra C. Duru

Victory And Fear Don't Mix - Stop Hiding!

I'm sure that by now, you're well aware that it's always said that fortune favors the brave, right? What if I told you that it goes even deeper than today?

Success and victory are not attainable in fear and timidity because they come through taking calculated risks, and fearful people never take any risks - calculated or brash. This is why they never experience true victory or success in their lives.

Day 33

"Fear has killed more dreams than failure: Many people have died and will keep dying with unfulfilled potential because they think they "can't" achieve their goals because of fear. You can and should do better!" - Dr.Sandra C. Duru

Your Dreams Are Achievable - Believe Nothing Else!

Do you know that the first step to achieving any goal, vision, purpose, or dream in life is to believe that it can be done and you can pull it off?

This is why the first thing the enemy also attacks in you is your faith, convictions, self-belief, and determination to see it to the end. One of the most efficient ways he does this is by planting fear and doubt in and around you.

Stop falling for this age-old trap that has sent many to the grave with all their dreams and purposes unfulfilled. Your dreams, visions, goals, and purpose are achievable. Believe nothing else, and you will see them to fruition!

Day 34

"Fear will keep you from trying: If you don't try, you lose every chance to succeed. Life is the survival of the fittest. Stand up and fight today!"
- Dr. Sandra C. Duru

You Can't Kill If You Don't Shoot - Keep Fighting!

One of my favorite hunters' quotes has been around for ages and still rings true: "You cannot kill if you don't shoot because only those who sow can reap."

Only those who don't give up and never stop fighting end up with the greatest good in life; fear is the greatest enemy of such courage. Kill it, and you will exceed any limitations in and around your life!

Day 35

"You should celebrate when you are plagued on every side with many battles and trials because it is a sign that you have a great destiny to fulfill." - Dr. Sandra C. Duru

Great Destinies Face Great Obstacles - Rejoice In Them!

I know that this may sound like an absolutely crazy thing to do. Still, do you know you're supposed to be jubilant and elated instead of being sad and deflated amid torrid battles against you?

Yes, you should be because the fierceness of the battles, oppositions, and obstacles against you is more than enough proof that you are destined for amazingly great things in life. And you will not be denied of your destiny as long as you do not throw in the towel and quit along the way.

Day 36

"The enemy doesn't come against those who don't have an assignment but attacks those on a mission and with significant projects. Unique destinies are prone to attacks." - Dr. Sandra C. Duru

The More Unique Your Destiny, The More Attacks & Enmity You Will Face!

Someone once asked me why I always spend a lot of time discussing battles, obstacles, tribulations, and how to overcome them, and my answer was straight and simple.

What you have is all you can give in life! Having been through some of the most brutal and darkest battles, my purpose is to let those coming behind me know that their tribulations and situations are not curses.

Instead, those dark times you're battling through today confirm the greatness the Creator deposited inside you. The more unique your destiny is, the more hostility and attacks you will suffer, so brace yourself, my dear champion. This will be a long ride, but rest assured, you will overcome it!

Day 37

"You are already endowed with everything you would ever need to make it through all the trials, attacks, persecutions, tribulations, and battles you must face on your path to your glorious destiny. Look inwards!" - Dr.Sandra C. Duru

You Have All It Takes Already - Stay On It!

Do you know that there is nothing you need to overcome any battle, obstacle, or trial that the Creator hasn't endued you with already?

HE said that HE would never allow you to be tempted beyond what you can bear, and HIS Word is infallible! No matter how enormous that obstacle before you may seem, it would never have been allowed to come against you if you could not overcome it.

Day 38

"Afflictions are the markers that let you know the possibilities and greatness ahead of you. The greater the affliction you must endure, the greater the destiny and testimony that awaits you!" - Dr. Sandra C. Duru

The Greater Your Afflictions, The Greater Your Testimonies - Stay Strong!

There is a level of understanding we must come into for many things to work better. Not because they would suddenly become easier but because they would be much more bearable.

One such is the understanding that the greater your trials and afflictions in life, the more immense your victories, glory, and testimonies will be if you do not relent and throw the towel halfway. Stay strong, my dear friend. It will not be in vain!

Day 39

"Always remember that just as you woke up today and started functioning without restrictions or bias of any kind, your success or greatness is not affected by any other factor but you!" - Dr. Sandra C. Duru

Nothing Can Stop Or Affect Your Success But You!

There is a fundamental truth that everyone should be told repeatedly from birth until they are mature enough to stand on their own.

It is the truth that nothing and no one else can stop or affect your success if you have not conceded defeat and accepted being tagged a failure. The only factor that can determine how your life will turn out, in the long run, is you, so you must never look down on yourself, no matter what your life looks like today!

Day 40

"Anyone can be great, rich, successful, and wealthy. There is no limit to what you can achieve no matter your gender!" - Dr. Sandra C. Duru

Wealth & Success Knows No Gender - Don't Be Discouraged!

Many people worldwide have been conditioned to believe that their potential and abilities are restricted by their gender. This is because of their parents, families, and societies' roles as they grew and their minds developed.

However, I would have you know today that there is no such limitation or gender bias regarding success and greatness. It is a fallacy birthed by ignorance, and you must break free from it to achieve your potential and purpose in life.

Day 41

"Not every person who offers you counsel has your interest or wellbeing at heart. Some are evil people whose only goal is to mislead as many unfortunate enough to approach them for counsel. A word, they say, is enough for the wise!" - Dr. Sandra C. Duru

Beware Of Advisors & Counselors - Keep Your Life Private!

Do you know that many people are swift to offer you counsel, not because they care about you genuinely, but because they're keen to mislead you so they can laugh at you when you fail?

Yes. Many are just evil people whose only goal is to mislead as many as are unfortunate enough to approach them for counsel. Hence, you must learn to keep your life, struggles, victories, testimonies, and even pains private.

Day 42

"Anxiety doesn't produce anything good. Anxiety does nothing to improve things when you are anxious about a situation, something, or an issue in life. Learn to shut it out of your mind by dwelling on positive thoughts and faith only." - Dr. Sandra C. Duru

Anxiety And Worry Are Counter-Productive - Flee From Them!

It is common and almost expected for a human to worry and get anxious about things that are out of our reach and control, especially when we need them.

However, do you know that worry and anxiety are not only counter-productive but also quite detrimental to you in many ways as they cannot solve your problem but will instead increase your blood pressure and stress levels? The most fantastic favor you can do for yourself is to avoid these two things diligently!

Day 43

"I am created for a purpose. Whether you want me or not, accept me or not, love me or not, and whether you are coming with me, I must fulfill my purpose." - Dr. Sandra C. Duru

You Are Created For A Purpose - Nothing Must Derail You!

Do you know that no matter how many friends, relatives, family, fans, associates, and all you have while on earth, no one will be there with you when you answer and give an account for all you did in life before our Creator?

This is why you must never allow anyone's sentiments, hatred, love, support, castigations, or whatever else they throw at you to derail or stop you from pursuing your dreams. You are created for a purpose, and it must be fulfilled!

Day 44

"Your destiny may seem complicated, but you cannot miss your purpose in life because you have a unique destiny, and you're one of a kind." - Dr. Sandra C. Duru

You Are One Of A Kind - You Can Never Be Destroyed!

Every new dawn and day we experience ought to be one that we begin with an affirmation that is not only true but very infallible too - Your destiny can only be delayed but never destroyed!

As much as I seem to say this consistently, I want to repeat to you today that you were created for a purpose, my dear, and no matter what happens, that plan of the Creator can never fail!

Hence, you should approach and tackle each day with a mind of victory and the spirit of a champion, knowing full well that nothing can surmount or defeat you.

Day 45

"If you take what narcissists do personally, you grant them real estate in your mind and psyche—which is exactly what they seek. Ignore them completely!" - Dr. Sandra C. Duru

Never Let Negative People Live Rent-Free In Your Head - Ignore Them!

Do you know there is no way negativity and evil can thrive in your life if you don't make your life and space accessible for them?

Yes, we are the ones who make ourselves victims and give narcissists the power to make our lives difficult and impossible. Never allow anyone to have that kind of power over your life. Ignore every negative energy and guard your space jealously always.

Day 46

"Being compassionate or empathetic does not mean that you should allow other people to demean and take undue advantage of you. Choosing to take good care of yourself is not narcissism but healthy living." - Dr. Sandra C. Duru

Taking Care And Looking Out For Yourself Is Not Narcissism - Don't Be Bullied!

There are many ways manipulative people take advantage of others around them who are soft-willed and are sadly ignorant of their ill intentions and evil ways.

One such is to make you believe that standing up for yourself and refusing to be treated like thrash is you being rebellious and narcissistic. However, this is false, and you should never allow yourself to be played and manipulated like this.

Day 47

"When you have a vision, you will become the vision bearer, and you must take your time to make your vision better and more precise. This would help you envision your mission and set proper goals and objectives to realize your vision." - Dr. Sandra C. Duru

The Vision Is Yours - No One Else Can Interpret It Better!

When the scriptures said to "write the vision and make it plain, that they may run with it that readeth it," the Creator was making something vital very plain to us all - your vision is unique to you, and no one else can ever interpret it better than you!

Hence, you must stop worrying about all the naysayers and even those always lurking around to steal your ideas. Instead, focus on what has been deposited inside you and seek the best ways to extract maximum and premium value from it for others.

Therein lies your fulfillment and the ultimate goal we should always strive for.

Day 48

"You may encounter some challenges in pursuing your dreams but do not be quick to give up on your vision. Nobody ever said that anything in life would be easy!" - Dr. Sandra C. Duru

Nothing In Life Comes Easy - Don't Let Go!

If there is anything that is assured and well-guaranteed in this life, it is the fact that we will all have troubles and face one persecution or the other as we continue to strive towards fulfilling our dreams and goals.

However, please remember that HE said that even though we have these issues and challenges that threaten to overpower us, we must never quit because we can never be forsaken!

Day 49

"Always focus on your vision and remain confident in pursuing your dreams. The challenges you see or encounter are part of the building process to actualizing your dreams. You will achieve your dream when you don't give up on it." - Dr. Sandra C. Duru

You Can't Reach Your Goals Without Obstacles - Run Through Them!

Do you know that there will always be many obstacles, trials, and tribulations constantly rising in your way as you seek to fulfill the purpose of God for you here on earth? This is a given, and there is nothing you or anyone else can do about it.

However, you have the power over the decision not to give up on your goals and dreams, no matter what rises against you. Understand that they're all part of your refining process and will end in praise soon if you don't quit on yourself.

Day 50

"The road to greatness is always rough and tough, but the gains that await you at your final destination far outweigh anything you must suffer along the way." - Dr. Sandra C. Duru

Growth And Pain Come Hand In Hand - Embrace It!

Have you ever considered the process that a grain of corn passes through before it can become a whole stick with many ears of corn?

The Master outlined this very simply and showed us why we must never be afraid to go through pain and rejection on our path to our desired greatness and destinies.

HE said, "Except a grain of wheat first falls to the ground and dies, it abides alone." Do you want to be exceptionally great and fruitful in your ways? Be ready for the process, for there is no growth without pain!

Day 51

"Don't be quick to abandon your dreams, ideas, vision, or projects, but be dogged and ensure you birth them. You can do it!" - Dr. Sandra C. Duru

Your Dreams Will Only Die If You Let Them - Never Relent!

Do you know what my ministry and goal as a person are? It is to inspire, educate, motivate, and empower many worldwide not to think of quitting on their dreams, purpose, and goals in life. Have I had it smooth and easy-going in life, too? Absolutely not!

I draw daily from the wealth and wells of experiences I've accumulated from countless battles, trials, and victories over the years. I assure you today that your life, too, can become a massive source of inspiration and motivation for millions worldwide, but only if you don't quit!

Like I have always done and still do, you must remain dogged, resilient, and determined to ensure your vision, purpose, and dreams are birthed.

Day 52

"Just because someone helped you in the past doesn't mean you are indebted to them for life. You cannot mortgage your future to appease the insecurities of your so-called friend." - Dr. Sandra C. Duru

Never Sacrifice Your Dreams To Appease Anyone - They Are Not Your God!

Man's inhumanity to his fellow man is not an evil that began today or recently. It has always been a part of human existence for the perceived stronger to lord their strengths over the weaker ones.

However, you must realize that no human being is your God, and no matter what anyone does for you, they must never take HIS place as the one you worship! Always remember that anyone who truly cares about you will never seek to enslave you because of any good they've done for you. Be wise!

Day 53

"Don't shrink yourself to make someone feel comfortable. You are allowed to grow and outgrow your friends from the past. Don't keep yourself stuck in the past because you want to be loyal to anyone." - Dr.Sandra C. Duru

Don't Kill Yourself For Anyone Else To Live - You Are Not A Slave!

There are times in everyone's lives when we all need a helping hand and a firm shoulder to cry and lean on through the troubles. And seeing anyone come through for you at such dreary times is a blessing.

However, no one should ever lord or hold that over your head and seek to perpetually keep you under them because they were there for you in your weakness or times of need.

You don't have to, and you must never sacrifice your life, career, future, destiny, and purpose to please, appease, or satisfy such sinister people!

Day 54

"Choose friends that reflect the future you aspire to. Never dumb down on your intelligence because you have surrounded yourself with people from your past. Your association in life also greatly determines how far you can go and what you'll achieve in it." - Dr. Sandra C. Duru

Your Friends And Associates Rub Off On You - Choose Wisely!

Do you know that, no matter how strong-willed and independent you are, if you consistently roll with the wrong bunch of people, you will eventually become entangled in their corruption and wrongdoings?

It's an age long adage and wisdom of nature, and it surely won't become invalid in your case - any sheep that hangs out with dogs every day will eventually eat shit. The only way to avoid such negative influences is to avoid them altogether!

Day 55

"Don't use your energy to worry about who likes or dislikes you. Use it to believe, create, impact, heal, inspire, plan, increase, motivate, love, trust, grow, glow, shine, manifest, and live your purpose." - Dr. Sandra C. Duru

Everyone Can Never Like You - Don't Waste Time Hoping They Will!

No matter how good, righteous, kind, upright, generous, honorable, virtuous, and amiable you are, there will always be people around you who will hate you for no justifiable reason.

The day you know, accept, and begin to walk and work with this age long truth, you will have more peace as you go about your day-to-day affairs. Everyone can never like you, no matter what you do, so don't waste your time trying to make them change.

Day 56

"Nothing just happens. Everything you experience is designed to work for you and not against you, depending on how you view them." - Dr. Sandra C. Duru

Life Will Work For Or Against You - Your Perspective Determines Your Outcome!

Have you ever wondered or asked yourself why the same things that killed countless people would yet make many others wealthy and successful? One person may take a path and end up being destroyed, yet another takes it and is led to his purpose and fulfillment.

The truth is that nothing just happens in life, my dear friend. There is a reason for everything, and, depending on the perspective you choose to have in every situation, anything can work for your good and favor you in life if you patiently learn how to swing it.

Day 57

> "Everything in life happens for us and not to us. It's a friendly universe. Don't fight against situations that come to try or even tempt you. Go with the flow and thrive as you rise through it." - Dr. Sandra C. Duru

Don't Struggle When Trials And Temptations Rise - Thrive Through Them!

Are you aware that one of the greatest weapons the enemy uses against you are the elements of fear and panic? Once your enemy makes you panic and fear, you have already lost that battle!

However, when you learn to see obstacles, afflictions, trials, temptations, and pain as what they are - building and stepping stones to your destiny and greatness, you will undoubtedly thrive through and overcome them all.

Day 58

"Ensure that you always remain positive so that, instead of seeing battles, pain, and obstacles, you'll be seeing opportunities for growth, victories, and testimonies!" - Dr. Sandra C. Duru

A Positive Mind Gives You An Edge - Keep It Always!

My beloved friend, do you know that there is an unassailable advantage that always keeping a positive mind gives you above others? Yes, there is, and it is the key behind many great people's success stories.

A positive mind will always see a way out of any battles and obstructions before it. While others see obstacles, a positive mind only sees opportunities. Hence, those who embrace this mindset are always great and highly successful in all their endeavors.

Day 59

"For you to truly grow and start thriving in life, you must build yourself up to a point where you are as self-sufficient and self-reliant as you require natural companionship." - Dr. Sandra C. Duru

Build Yourself Up In Life - Be Your Own Companion

There is a fundamental law in life that many people ignore, and I dare say it is why there is so much pain and rejection all around us.

It states that to love another, you must first love yourself because what you don't have, you cannot give!

Hence, if you're honest about breaking new ground and growing exponentially in all your endeavors, you must learn to build yourself up and be your companion first.

Day 60

"Do good, and good will come to you. Don't ever allow how others maltreat you to affect your life. You can change your situation and that of your loved ones. All you need to do is take a bold step of faith." -Dr. Sandra C. Duru

Faith Is All You Need To Change Your Life - Keep Doing Good!

Are you aware that you can change your situation and that of your loved ones by taking a bold step of faith and never allowing doubt to keep you down?

The Master said that all you need is "faith as a mustard seed," and you will move mountains and do those seemingly impossible things you had never thought you could with ease.

Day 61

"Life is like a long queue that we are all on and, sooner or later, each of us will move on that queue till we get to the points of our rest, peace, unlimited love and goodness, and God's reserved blessings for us. Be patient!" - Dr. Sandra C. Duru

Everyone On Life's Queue Will Get Their Blessings - Be Patient!

Sometimes, we look all around us and feel like we're being left behind because everyone seems to be making progress and getting blessed but us. My dear friend, this cannot be farther from the truth than it is.

God has no child HE does not have a plan for, and none of us will be left behind in HIS goodness and blessings. HE that gives rain to both the righteous and the wicked, shall HE now refrain from doing good to those who trust, believe in, and love HIM?

Day 62

"You do not need everyone to be happy and fulfilled in life. People meant to be in your life will be there when it's time for them to return."
- Dr. Sandra C. Duru

Know People's Time And Phase In Your Life - You Don't Need Everybody!

Are you aware that God makes provisions for all HIS children and places different people in their lives for various purposes at different phases?

No one can stay with you and be relevant to your life forever unless they were specially gifted to you by God. The day you understand this, you will stop bothering about everyone around you and learn to focus on the right people who are destined to go all the way with you.

Day 63

"Barrenness is not your inability to turn around your situation or recreate your story. Don't let society judge you and send you into depression." - Dr. Sandra C. Duru

Barrenness Is Not Akin To Childlessness - Don't Accept Negative Tags!

One of the biggest challenges and evils any couple can experience in many African countries, especially women, is the issue of childlessness. This is a very sensitive topic, and many have been erringly tagged as "barren" because of this.

However, a childless person is not the barren one but the one who cannot adapt, recreate themselves, and turn around their life in any situation they find themselves. This is because even the Creator has already given us "all that pertains to life (childbearing, fruitfulness, etc.) and godliness"!

Day 64

"Hope is the one thing that can help you get through the darkest times, storms, tough moments, and situations. It is never over until you throw in the towel, so you must remain hopeful and keep fighting even when it looks like you've lost the battle." - Dr. Sandra C. Duru

It's Never Over Till You Quit - Keep Fighting Champion!

Are you aware that there are many definitions of some words we learned while growing up, which may affect us negatively today? One such is the definition of what it means to "fail" or be a "failure" in life.

Do you know that trying to do or accomplish something and not getting it right or done does not make you a failure, no matter how often it happens? Yes, my dear friend, you only truly fail when you lose hope and allow yourself to believe you are worthless.

Day 65

"When faced with difficult situations, you must act rather than brood over your condition. Don't die in silence, and don't allow depression to set in. Be hopeful." - Dr. Sandra C. Duru

Worrying Never Solves Problems - Only Action Does!

By how humans are wired by nature, it is pretty standard to get worried when things don't go as planned or when there is much uncertainty about our hopes, plans, and dreams.

However, do you know that worrying about things or getting anxious does not solve or help you in any situation? Instead, it multiplies your challenges by magnifying the issues and making them seem insurmountable.

Day 66

"Be hopeful and patient, and remain strong. It is never over for you until you throw in the towel and give up. You will be fine if you do not quit." - Dr. Sandra C. Duru

Failure Only Occurs When You Quit - You Must Persevere!

My dear friend, do you know that there are many things we never get right the first time we try them but eventually get done and move on as if nothing happened?

I'm here to tell you today that there is no difference between them and those projects, dreams, visions, and pursuits many have labeled you a failure.

All you need is to focus on your goals, ignore the several shortcomings and falls along the way, and keep pushing toward the mark, and very soon those same mouths that derided you will come to celebrate you!

Day 67

"No matter how far you seem to have fallen in life, you are not a victim or an object of pity!" - Dr. Sandra C. Duru

Never Let The Enemy's Gloating Get To You - You Are A Champion!

I love a verse in the scriptures so much because it has always supported me through every phase and season of battles and fierce opposition.

The Prophet Micah said: "Rejoice not against me, O mine enemy: when I fall, I shall arise; when I sit in darkness, the LORD shall be a light unto me." - Micah 7:8.

I share this with you today because I need you to understand a profound truth about yourself. You were created to excel, dominate, subdue, and replenish the earth wherever you go. You are not a weakling, and none can trample you under their feet unless you allow them!

Day 68

"You have the right to stay away from toxic people and environments. You have the right to decide to be happy and maintain a healthy mindset all the time. You don't and should never need anyone's permission to do this." - Dr. Sandra C. Duru

A Happy And Healthy Mind Is Your Right - Don't Be Denied!

My beloved friend, are you aware that you have the power and exclusive right to determine and decide what should happen to you at every phase and stage of your life?

You are not a victim of fate or circumstances, and the Creator did not put you at the mercy of any other created being. Hence, you must never be made to feel like you need anyone's permission to have a healthy mindset or to be happy in life.

Day 69

"Broken people will always break others around them, too, because all they know and have inside them is brokenness. You cannot give what you don't have, remember?" - Dr. Sandra C. Duru

Be Wary Of The Company You Keep - Hurt People Cannot Give Anything But Pain!

Have you ever had people around you who never seemed to have anything good or positive to say or contribute to everything happening and all they see?

Such people are always bitter about everything; nothing good grows or thrives around them. Hanging around or keeping them in your life guarantees you will continue having avoidable toxic drama, needless squabbles, and unwanted negativity. Please, don't do that to yourself!

Day 70

"Never draw the curtain on a year when the year is yet to draw the curtain on itself. Who says it's ever too late to achieve a purpose and goal you have a well-laid plan for? - Dr. Sandra C. Duru

It's Never Too Late To Achieve Your Goals - Your Time Will Come

Do you know that there is a time appointed to everyone on earth to break even and prosper in whatever our pursuits are?

The Creator has a plan for each of us, and in HIS time, HE will make all that concerns you "beautiful," according to HIS word!

The onus now lies with you to never despair, lose focus, or ever quit on your pursuits and God-given purpose, no matter the type or level of opposition that rises against you.

Day 71

"There are lots of grounds to be watered, and there will always be countless opportunities to achieve things in this life. The only thing required of you is never to become redundant and always be on the move." - Dr. Sandra C. Duru

Yesterday's Victories Do Not Guarantee Success Today - Keep Grinding!

Have you ever wondered why there is always a battle for the same trophy and title one team wins in a sports league immediately after another season or year begins?

One would think that since they've been crowned as the best team, every other team should not bother competing against them anymore, right? However, the reality is hugely far from this, and the reason is simple, my dear friend.

No king rules his empire, keeps it safe from invaders, or even retains his crown based on yesterday's victories. A victor yesterday may suffer heavy defeat and be dethroned today if he ever gets complacent and stops grinding and working as hard as he used to before his previous successes. Never fall into this trap!

Day 72

"There will never be a "good" or "perfect" time to start anything you want to do in life. There will only be now, and your resolve to achieve your purpose should be your driving force and motivation daily." - Dr. Sandra C. Duru

The Only Time You Have Is Now - Just Do It!

One of my all-time favorite marketing lines by any company remains the world-renowned line by Nike: "Just do it!" Besides how catchy this phrase is, there are so many hidden motivational lessons, but let me share a major one with you today.

No matter the obstacles, oppositions, and limitations standing in the way of any project, dream, or vision you have, never be swayed or dismayed by their enormity or their constant taunts that you will fail if you move. Just do it!

Waiting to have enough resources, or when other factors favor you, is an age long trap the enemy has always used to stagnate and eventually kill many dreams and visions. That "right time" will never come because you're in it already. Take action now!

Day 73

"If you want to reach your potential and improve your mental health, you have to take control of your inner voice and learn how to tame it and transform it into a positive force." - Dr. Sandra C. Duru

Transform Your Mind Into A Positive Force - Your Life Depends On It!

There is a story in the scriptures that I love so much. It describes what happened when Joshua, Caleb, and the other ten spies who went into Canaan returned to Moses and Israel with their report.

Many people panicked and uttered careless words out of fear, and God held them accountable for those idle words. Why? It's because they allowed their minds to drift away from HIM and become filled with fear despite all the great wonders God had wrought before and for them along that journey.

No matter what comes up against you, always ensure your mind stays positive, and your eyes remain on HIM alone. The quality and type of life you will have here on earth depends on this very vital act!

Day 74

"Be conscious about what you're putting in your head. The first step to unlocking your mind power is to remove thoughts with negative emotions completely. This means removing negative self-talk and setting aside fear." - Dr. Sandra C. Duru

Negative Self-Talk And Fear Are Your Enemies - Get Rid Of Them!

My dear friend, have you ever seen anyone trying to fill a tank with water but first drill many big holes at the base? Even the thought of it is weird to you right now, isn't it?

Well, what if I told you this is what you do to yourself daily whenever you allow fear and negative self-talk to govern your thoughts and actions? Nothing good and positive can grow or thrive in such a negative mind, and you must help yourself by getting rid of them today.

Day 75

"There is nothing like the right time to start doing the right things for your health and happiness and get the best results. Move now!" -Dr. Sandra C. Duru

There Is Never A "Right Time" To Take Care Of Yourself - It Is Now!

Hello friends, how're you doing today? Are you aware there is never a better or "perfect time" to look after your health and well-being than now?

Putting things off and waiting for the "right time" to do them is why many people hardly ever get anything good done almost all through their lives! Don't fall into that trap, too. And, if you've been living like that before, now is the perfect time to get up and turn your life around...today!

Day 76

"All we have in life is time, and you can choose to make it right or wrong. Yes, there's no right time, but time! All you have is time and what you choose to do with it." - Dr. Sandra C. Duru

Time Is All You Have - Use It Well!

Are you aware that one of the most significant differences between the super-wealthy and those who are very poor is time and how they spend it?

This is a significant determinant of what we will become and achieve - how we spend our time and what we love doing daily.

The Creator gave every one of us this gift called time in equal measure. We all have 24 hours daily, and your life, situation, position, and condition today directly reflect how you've spent your time in all the yesterdays you've had.

Day 77

"The time is now. Don't ever think of giving up on your plans, visions, and goals because you think it's not the best or the right time." - Dr. Sandra C. Duru

What Time Is It Best To Pursue Your Dreams?

My darlings, how are you all doing today? Do you know there is never a better time to pursue your goals, dreams, visions, and purpose in life than right now, even as you're reading this?

A very wise king once said: "A living dog is better than a dead lion," and the reason is pretty simple - once dead and in the grave, all hopes, abilities, and possibilities of ever achieving anything again in life are gone.

So, when is the best time to pursue your dreams, goals.

Day 78

"Don't quit simply because it's impossible to do it now. Maybe you have to make the time right, and you will succeed. Don't lose hope. You're on the right track. It will happen at the right time and season." - Dr. Sandra C. Duru

Things Will Happen For You In Their Appointed Time - Never Lose Hope!

My beloved darling, I trust your day has started beautifully today. I have a short word of encouragement for you today, and I know it will lift your spirit as always.

Are you aware that there is an appointed time for everything under the sun, and no matter how long it may seem to take, your time and blessings will undoubtedly come, too?

Never let anyone make you feel useless, worthless, or inadequate because your time has not come yet. This is the only reason things seem not to be working presently, but don't ever lose hope because your time is coming, and great things will also start to happen for you.

Day 79

"There is no such thing as a perfect time; now is the time. Many people are connected to that dream, so please don't kill it with procrastination. Don't condemn the numerous destinies connected to you to a long wait; act now!" - Dr. Sandra C. Duru

Stop Killing Your Dreams With Procrastination - Act Now!

It's another beautiful week to be alive, and I'm glad to be able to share this day with you again today, my dear friend.

Have you ever been told that you were not created for yourself alone, and there are countless destinies connected to you who are eagerly praying for your success and lifting so that they can start prospering, too?

Yes, my dear. Your dream, vision, goal, and purpose are connected to many other destinies worldwide. Hence, you must cast aside everything that keeps you down, especially any act of procrastination, which is the chief destroyer of every good dream and purpose.

Day 80

"Many people do not like seeing others happy or you doing well. A lot of people have been killed by their friends out of envy, hatred, and jealousy. Be careful!" - Dr. Sandra C. Duru

Many Have Died From So-Called Friends - Be Careful!

My beloved friends, how are you doing today? I hope your week has been good so far.

Do you know that there are many people in an early grave today who have no business being there yet because they were initially supposed to live long and fulfilling lives?

Yes, many have died before their time because they were not mindful of the kind of people they let into their lives as friends, associates, and even lovers. You must always be extremely careful of those you open yourself up to. Judas was also one of the 12 and an Apostle, remember?

Day 81

"Keep shining on and doing well on your lane. If you have done well and still doing excellently well in life, it's not bragging. So never dim your light for no one!" - Dr. Sandra C. Duru

If You've Worked For It, Be Proud Of It - That's Not Bragging!

excellent health and shape today.

Do you know it is wrong for anyone to make you feel like you're doing bad things by celebrating your wins and victories?

Many people will try to gaslight you into thinking you're being "proud" for giving yourself some much-needed pats on the back for your great efforts, but you must never let them do this to you. Stand your ground, and stand firm against such devious manipulations!

Day 82

"You need to get a mind that works like a sieve and filter every word you hear. Think before you speak any word out of your mouth. Discern every spirit and weigh every association you keep!" - Dr. Sandra C. Duru

Be Wary Of The Association You Keep - Test All Spirits!

Greetings, my darling. How are you faring this beautiful day? Are you aware that you are majorly judged by many people who meet you for the first time based on several things, and the company you keep is vital?

Also, do you know that you're not expected to follow and swallow everything any counselor or "wise person" tells you without putting those words to the ultimate litmus test, the Word of God?

My darling, you must test every spirit around you and also be very wary of the kind of company you keep. These two things will save you from numerous untold hardships and deliver you from avoidable troubles all your life.

Day 83

"Don't ever believe their lies that you are not worth it. Don't ever believe that you're a 'nobody.' Do not believe the fallacies that there is no need to stretch a little further and leave your comfort zone." - Dr. Sandra C. Duru

Evil People Will Always Create Lies About You - Believing Them Is Up To You.

My darling friend, have you ever wondered why some people have tried and continue trying to break you down and convince you that you're worthless?

I have a simple question that will liberate your mind from their wickedness for you today: If you were so worthless, useless, and a no-good, why have they been putting so much effort into destroying you? Why do they keep having sleepless nights as you progress through life if you are genuinely as useless as they try to make you believe?

See, my darling, evil people will always make up terrible lies, accusations, and derogatory stories about you to break your morale and destroy your mind. It is now up to you to choose whether to believe the enemy's lies about you or to keep your eyes on God's report, which is HIS Word. The choice is yours!

Day 84

"Your glory and destiny are not determined by your geographical location but by the content you carry and how well you nurture and maximize it." - Dr. Sandra C. Duru

Your Content Determines Your Blessings, Not Your Location!

My beloved darlings, how are you doing today? Has anyone ever told you that if you are a fish in a pond, you can never automatically become an alligator if someone drops you in a lake?

Yes, my dear friend. Your greatness, glory, blessings, and success are more dependent and determined by your gifts, talents, and abilities than your location. Hence, you need to focus and work more on discovering, building, and developing your content than you do on changing your location in life.

Day 85

"There is so much potential in you that you won't believe there is. Stretch some more...your point of elasticity is unlimited!" - Dr. Sandra C. Duru

You Have No Breaking Point - You Only Need To Believe!

Hello, my beautiful darlings. I trust that you had a splendid night's rest. I have a short word of encouragement for you today.

Are you aware that your so-called "point of elasticity" is infinite, and you have zero limits because you are HIS creation and child? Yes, God made you in HIS image and likeness.

Now, If the one who created and formed you in HIS likeness has no limits or impossibilities, how or why should you think you do? That would mean HE lied about making you in HIS likeness, and God cannot lie!

Day 86

"You are your only limitation, and you will only grow to the point that you allow yourself to stretch to in life!" - Dr. Sandra C. Duru

The Only Thing Stopping You Is You - There Are No Limits!

My beloved friends, how are you doing today?

As many times as I may have said these words to you, they still ring very true, and I will put them out here again today because someone still needs to hear and believe them genuinely.

Man (not gender specific) was made in the image and likeness of God, his Creator; hence, man has no limits whatsoever! There are no bounds and limits you cannot overcome and surpass. The only thing stopping you in life is you!

Day 87

"Success and goodness are always attracted to a kind of demeanor, spirit, and countenance that victors carry about themselves consistently. Whatever you are going through today, you must remain strong, calm, resilient, confident, and focused." - Dr. Sandra C. Duru

There Is A Mindset That Attracts Success - Develop And Dwell On It!

Hello, my beloved friend. I hope your day has started pleasantly today.

Do you know that success and goodness are like spirits and are always only attracted to a particular mindset, countenance, and mental outlook? Yes, they are!

At the risk of sounding like a broken record, I must remind you again today: Your mind is a powerful magnet that attracts anything it consistently dwells on into your life. If all you think of is failure, poverty, sickness, and other negative things, you shouldn't expect to experience anything different from them.

Day 88

" No matter what you may think you could get out of it, you don't ever have to live a false life. It is way too toxic and draining and never ends well. Avoid it!" - Dr. Sandra C. Duru

Living A False Life Never Ends Well - Avoid It!

Hello, my darling friend. Are you aware you are so unique that no one else could ever be you?

This is how much the Creator invested in you to ensure you live an outstanding and incredibly fulfilling life here.

However, when you choose to become a copy of someone else, lie to yourself and others around you, and pretend to be what and who you're not, you not only dishonor HIM but also do yourself a huge disservice!

Day 89

"Any situation, circumstances, or person that tries to force you into being what and who you are not is not a good thing or place for you to be. You must never compromise your values and identity to suit or please any other person's agenda." - Dr. Sandra C. Duru

Never Compromise Your Values For Anything - Nothing Is Worth Your Dignity!

My beloved friend, I trust your day has started well today and your week has been splendid.

My words for you today are in continuance of what I've been trying to get you to understand for a few days now profoundly, and I hope you are taking everything to heart.

There is nothing on this planet that is worth devaluing yourself over. You must never compromise your values and identity to suit or please any other person's agenda!

Day 90

"Know your self-worth, understand your uniqueness and purpose in life, and only stick around those who accept and help you grow genuinely."
- Dr. Sandra C. Duru

Don't Hang Around Anyone Who Doesn't Help You Grow - Value Yourself More!

Hello, my wonderful friend. How are you today? Have you ever been told that constantly being around people who are never interested in your growth is pretty harmful and self-destructive?

My dear, you have no business keeping such people around you or even staying in their circles, no matter what they try to entice you with. Your destiny and God-given purpose are way bigger than anything anyone can ever offer to keep you in one spot. Hence, you need to value yourself more today genuinely!

QUARTERLY SELF-APPRAISAL | REVIEW

(1) List three things you feel you excelled at this quarter.

(2) What were your primary goals this quarter, and did you get started on any of them?

(3) How many of your goals, dreams, and objectives did you achieve this quarter?

(4) On a scale of 1-10, rate the level of success you've been able to achieve this quarter, and why you think you deserve your allotted mark.

(5) What would you consider to be your most significant achievement this quarter?

QUARTER 2:

DAY 91 - DAY 181

Day 91

"Friendship is not always about surrounding yourself with people who always agree. The inside and the outside can be two different stories, so you should learn to embrace individual differences." - Dr. Sandra C. Duru

Embrace Individual Differences - This Is The Beauty Of Friendship

Hi there, my beloved friend.

There are a few things in life that you can find succor and draw strength from in the day of trials and afflictions, and one of them is the association you keep. Friends are invaluable in such times, especially if they're good and Godly ones!

However, as you relate and socialize with people, it is essential to know that everyone is unique, and we cannot all think and act the same way. Hence, you must learn to accommodate these differences and never allow them to brew conflicts in your relationships with your friends and loved ones.

Day 92

"Learn to become one with your intuition, spirit, and the discernment that nudges at you from within on many things around you most times. You would naturally overcome many obstacles and unforeseen challenges if you're in tune with your inner spirit and stop resisting its flow and directions." - Dr. Sandra C. Duru

No Obstacle Can Prevail Over You If You Are In Tune With Your Inner Spirit - Listen More!

My beloved darling, how are you today? Do you know that the primary reason why the enemy keeps attacking your mind and keeps trying hard to distort your thoughts is that he understands the kind of power inherent in it?

He also knows the damage you can do to him and all his works once you are in tune with your inner spirit and feeding it with the right words, instructions, and inspirations.

Hence, he will stop at nothing to ensure you don't because he knows you will naturally overcome many obstacles and unforeseen challenges if you're in tune with your inner spirit and stop resisting its flow and directions.

Day 93

"Your present scene is only a small part of the story that will be told of how you braved all odds against you and came out victorious if you do not quit on yourself along the way." - Dr. Sandra C. Duru

Today's Battles Are Tomorrow's Testimonies - Don't Stop Pushing!

My beloved darlings, do you know that the way you went through all your travails, battles, and trials now will become the story and legend many will hear about you tomorrow?

Yes, the going is incredibly tough and rough presently, but you should never think of quitting. You will come out victorious sooner than you think, and your life's story, too, will become an inspiration and source of motivation for countless people worldwide.

Day 94

"There is still much more to your story than you're experiencing right now, and you cannot afford to throw in the towel just yet! Those that we celebrate today are the ones who kept fighting on against all odds."
- Dr. Sandra C. Duru

You Must Never Quit If You Want To Be Celebrated, Too - That's The Way Life Works!

Greetings, my dear friends. How are you doing today? I know you have always longed to be an accomplished and celebrated success in your career and business pursuits, but do you know there is a small price to pay for this?

And this is not a one-time payment like when you go into a store to purchase goods. It is a price you must pay consistently and never slack on because it simply requires that you show up, keep fighting, and never settle for less in your life daily.

Day 95

"When you don't bring others down to be the number one, and you wait patiently on God Almighty with faith, patience, and hard work, you will become successful in life, and your blessings will be permanent." - Dr. Sandra C. Duru

You Shouldn't Destroy Others To Rise - There Is Plenty Of Room For All!

My beloved friends, I trust that your day has started well today.

As you go about your day, I want you to learn and hold on to this significant truth.

If you ever have to pull down, tarnish, or destroy someone else to acquire anything or get any promotion in life, what you have achieved is not success but a curse because it is undoubtedly not of or from God.

There is more than enough room for every one of us at the top, and you don't need to destroy anyone to make way or create space for yourself there - well, that's if you want your blessing to be genuine, lasting, and generational because it's from God, though.

Day 96

> "Don't ever kill to be famous or rich. Don't destroy others to climb higher than them. If you are destined for greatness and know who you are and your Father is, you will follow your path and be successful with a pure heart to the end." - Dr. Sandra C. Duru

If You Must Kill Others To Succeed, You Have Failed Instead - Don't Do It!

Greetings to you, my darlings. How is your day going today? Do you know that if you are destined for greatness and understand who you are and your Father is, you will follow your path and be successful with a pure heart to the end?

My dear, fishes don't struggle to swim inside water, nor do eagles struggle to glide upon the winds and hit altitudes no other birds would dare attempt. Why? It's in them - an innate, God-given ability and skill!

You were created and born a victorious success in life, and it is only a matter of time before all the Creator deposited inside you begins to manifest and yield fruits fully. However, if you impatiently run ahead of HIM and yourself and start to engage in nefarious activities in the name of "getting rich and being successful," have you truly succeeded or failed woefully? Selah!

Day 97

"Nobody can bring you down or destroy you if you don't give them the chance to do so. People will try to get you down by all means, but you can either go down, stay down, or stand up and keep moving." - Dr. Sandra C. Duru

You Have The Power To Decide What Brings You Down Or Not - You Are Not Helpless!

Have you ever been in a situation where it looked like you had no choice but to succumb to the enemy's attacks and be defeated?

Many of us have been there at one time or another, but some, like me, have always scaled through them excellently, and the reason is simple.

No matter how good or whatever you do in life, people will always try to get you down by all means. However, you can either go down, stay down, or stand up and keep moving. God has equipped you with all you need to survive and triumph over any obstacles in your path. So, what will you do today?

Day 98

"Do you know that the will to conquer is the first condition of victory? You don't have to be in doubt about your success, neither do you have to announce your success ahead of time. Talk less about your plans, and let your wins do the talking." - Dr. Sandra C. Duru

The Will To Conquer Precedes Victory - Develop It!

Greetings to you, my darling friend. How are you doing today? I have a short but powerful word of inspiration and motivation for you today, and I am confident it will bless you immensely.

Do you know that you cannot win in any situation unless you have a strong will never to lose? Those resigned to defeat before a fight can hardly come out as victors!

Likewise, you should never doubt your success, nor should you announce your success ahead of time. Talk less about your plans, and let your wins do the talking.

Day 99

"The act of judging comes from insecurity and is a symptom of unhappiness and bitterness. If you are truly happy, you don't need to cut others down to size or put down the choices others have made." – Dr. Sandra C. Duru

Judging Others Harshly Is A Sign Of A Disturbed Soul - Conquer Your Demons!

My wonderful friend, I hope your day has started splendidly.

Do you know that a genuinely happy person doesn't ever feel the need to belittle, tarnish, pull down, and destroy someone else's achievements or happiness to feel fulfilled or accomplished?

Please beware, my dear. Such desires and impulses reveal a deep-lying problem that must be addressed swiftly before it consumes you. If you are truly happy, you don't need to cut others down to size or put down their choices in any area of their lives.

Day 100

"True progress in life is almost always a slow process that requires you to move one tiny step at a time. Even God attested to this when HE said not to "despise the days of little beginnings." – Dr. Sandra C. Duru

Genuine Progress Is Never Speedy - Don't Despair!

My beloved friend, do you feel like all your efforts haven't yielded any tangible results, no matter how hard you've tried? I have a word of encouragement and motivation for you today.

No seed grows upwards first when it is planted; they always grow downwards before springing back up. Depending on how massive that plant will be, it may take much longer to go through this process before the farmer sees it sprouting on the surface.

This also applies to you if you must have any meaningful and genuine success in life, my dear. It always looks slow and sometimes nonexistent, but never despair or quit! Your time to break through will also come, so keep pushing and do not relent.

Day 101

"There is no slow progress in life. There is only progress. Whether running, flying, walking, or crawling, you are making progress as long you're headed in the right direction!" – Dr. Sandra C. Duru

You Are Making Progress As Long As You're Moving - Keep Going!

Hello, my beloved darlings. How are you doing today?

Do you know that many of us are the primary reason we easily get discouraged and depressed because we keep focusing on the wrongest things in our journey through life? Yes, we sadly hamstrung ourselves by comparing other people's speed to ours, forgetting that no two humans have the same destiny and process in life.

Please know and understand this well today, my dear. Whether running, flying, walking, or crawling, you are making progress as long you're headed in the right direction. So stop worrying unnecessarily and keep going!

Day 102

"Life is fascinating and sweet if only we have the passcode to our path. When we understand how best to live life, it becomes enjoyable and stress-free." – Dr. Sandra C. Duru

Your Life Can Be However You Want It - Live Free!

Hello, my beloved friends. I trust that your day has started well today. Do you know that many issues we create for ourselves give us avoidable and unnecessary stress?

Yes, my dear, and the major challenge stems from not being knowledgeable enough about many aspects of our daily lives. However, if you can find out how things work in detail before launching yourself into them, you'll be surprised at how easy many things in life are!

When you understand how best to live life, it becomes delightful and stress-free.

Day 103

"The bird dares to break the shell, then the shell breaks open, and the bird can fly openly. This is the simplest principle of success. You dream, you dare, you breakthrough, and then you fly." – Dr. Sandra C. Duru

If You Can't Dare, You Can't Succeed - Dare To Dream!

My darling friend, have you ever seen a hunter who goes into the forest with a loaded gun and refuses to let off a single shot but still comes home with plenty of game? If he does, then he must have indeed stolen them!

Life's sweetest rewards are available to all of God's creations, but only if you dare to dream and take the necessary steps to bring that dream, ambition, vision, purpose, or project to life. If you can't dare to do this, you can't succeed at anything in life. It's that simple!

Day 104

"War is peace...if you know how to conquer. Peace only genuinely exists when all enemies, tormentors, and evil people have all been subdued, silenced, or destroyed before you." – Dr. Sandra C. Duru

There Can Be No Peace Without War - Subdue Your Enemies!

My precious darling, has anyone ever told you there is no peace without war, for peace only genuinely exists when all enemies, tormentors, and evil people have all been subdued, silenced, or destroyed before you?

Yes, my darling, the only route to true and lasting peace is war because an enemy you leave breathing and growing today is a potential enormously giant destruction that can pounce upon you tomorrow!

Hence, you must never hesitate or be afraid to strike when you have the power, opportunity, and resources. Only then is your peace and future guaranteed - after all your enemies are subdued before you.

Day 105

"Anger and hatred that fuels rage and violence in people are very corrosive emotions – they destroy both the one who wields them and whatever they're used to target. Make up your mind to have no part in this destructive tendencies." – Dr. Sandra C. Duru

Hatred And Anger Destroy Both Ways - Don't Become Slaves To Them!

My beloved friends, how are you all doing today? Are you aware that hatred and anger are terrible emotions that destroy the one who wields them and whatever they're aimed at?

While it is human to feel these emotions when provoked or pushed to the wall by ingrates and evil people occasionally, you must ensure that you protect your mental health, mental toughness, and sanity by refusing to harbor hatred and anger towards anyone.

The enemy keeps whispering into your ears and constantly reminds you of the evil and wrongs people do against you because he wants to enslave you to these harmful emotions. He knows that his evil purpose for your life is fulfilled by so doing.

Hence, you must decide to have no part in this kind of destructive tendency. Please hand over all your pain and grief to God, and HE will not only soothe your heart but also fight your battles and grant you the vindication and victory you deserve.

Day 106

"Do you know that the will to conquer is the first condition of victory? Never doubt your success; neither should you announce your success ahead of time." - Dr. Sandra C. Duru

A Mind That Doubts Its Success Will Fail - Keep Believing!

My beloved friends, do you know some vital secrets about success that you must know before you can achieve the greatness and success the Creator has destined you for?

In all of humankind's history, it has never been recorded anywhere that there has ever been anyone with the will, burning desire, mental toughness, and faith that they could achieve any goals they set and failed. This is because nature is programmed to yield the earth's resources and success to such tenacious minds and will.

The same can and will be said and written about you, too, my dear. However, you must never doubt your success; neither should you announce your success beforehand. Keep your moves private and your heart filled with faith; in no time, your success and greatness shall announce themselves to the whole world!

Day 107

"You are so much more than you believe! You can triumph in any challenges of life without any fears. All you need to do is stay focused and always make plans for the long-term as much as you plan for today." - Dr. Sandra C. Duru

Always Plan For Tomorrow As Much As You Do For Today - Secure Your Future!

Hello, my darling. I trust you are well today.

Do you know that the only thing that can ever hinder your progress and success in life is a lack of belief and faith in yourself? Yes, my dear. You must be your number one fan and cheerleader because no other person can believe in you if you don't believe in yourself!

When you have this mindset, you are pretty much unstoppable, and all you need to do consistently is to remain focused on your dreams, purpose, and objectives. You must also always make plans for the long-term as much as you plan for today because it is essential to secure your future even as you take care of the present.

Day 108

"There is not one person or thing that is the key to your success. You are more than enough!" - Dr. Sandra C. Duru

You Were Created And Born A Success - You Are More Than Enough!

Hello, my darling. I hope your week has begun excellently. I have a short word of motivation for someone out there today, and I would love for you to understand this as clearly as possible.

When God said that HE would never share HIS glory with any man, it goes deeper beyond being God. It includes everything that happens to HIS precious creations, and you, my dear, are at the top of that order.

What am I saying to you today? It's simple: You were created and born to be a great success by God; hence, you don't need any human being or spirit to achieve this in life. You are more than enough, my dear, and you must never believe or settle for anything less than this truth!

God's unique love for you will never let HIM place your destiny in the hands of another created being, so you must realize and understand that you are the essential factor in the story and course of your life after HIM. Nothing and no one else matters more, so discover, develop, equip, and encourage yourself in your God-given purpose and dreams, and the sky will be but a starting point for you, darling.

Day 109

> "No other person can ever control your destiny but you! You are the best person to bring your idea to the market and introduce your dreams to the world." - Dr. Sandra C. Duru

You Are The Best Marketer Of Your Dreams - Push Them Now!

My beloved darlings, do you know that every man's dreams, goals, visions, and purpose in life are peculiar to him, and none on earth can ever interpret them well unless you expressly guide them as the owner of the dream?

Yes, you are the best person to bring your idea to the market and introduce your dreams to the world because nobody knows them better!

Hence, even God, our Creator, urges us to: "And the LORD answered me, and said, Write the vision, and make it plain upon tables, that he may run that readeth it." - Habakkuk 2:2.

If you don't put down your dreams and goals, they'll stay as mere wishes in your mind and may never come to fruition. So, please be bold and assured that you will never fail because you have already been endowed with everything you need to succeed, my darling! And also always remember that.

Day 110

"Failure is a stepping stone to success and greater achievements if you don't give up on yourself, your dreams, visions, goals, pursuits or become available to distractions, lies, negative energies, and unproductive ventures." - Dr. Sandra C. Duru

Failure Is Only A Momentary Pause - It Should Never Be Your End!

My dear friend, have you ever been told that delay is not denial and failure is not final in your journey and the quest for greatness in life? Yes, they are not, and unless you allow them to weigh you down, they are only temporary bleeps you shouldn't dwell on as you seek to fulfill your God-given purpose.

That you attempted to do something that didn't work out the first time doesn't mean it would never work or that you failed. You only fail when you quit and stop trying, and that's what the enemy always tries to get you to do - quit instead of pressing on!

Life is filled with too many examples of great men, women, inventors, kings, generals, business tycoons, and others who didn't get it right several times when they initially tried. However, they're all being celebrated today because they understand they can be considered failures only if they give up. Be inspired to continue pushing through no matter how often you falter, my darling, and you will be celebrated as a champion soon.

Day 111

"Don't ever change so people will like you. Be patient, keep being your amazing self, and soon the right people will love the real you." - Dr. Sandra C. Duru

It Is Not Love If You Have To Pretend To Earn It - You Deserve Better!

My lovely friends, I trust your week has been fantastic. I have a short word of motivation from Mother Nature for someone out there today, and I know it will significantly inspire you to be more and to do more with your life.

What is that thing or person you've desired and pursued for so long but they don't seem to be looking your way? Relax, keep calm, and never lose your self-worth, dignity, identity, and uniqueness to win them.

Anything you have to pretend, live a fake life, and start doing things contrary to your destiny to win for yourself is a considerable loss, plague, and a trap of the enemy to pervert and destroy your destiny and God-given purpose in life. Hence, you must avoid such with all diligence because it is not love and undoubtedly not genuine if you have to pretend or lie to obtain them.

Believe me, my darling; you surely deserve much better than that! So, just be patient, keep being your fabulous self, and pretty soon, the right people will love the real you.

Day 112

"You don't need other people to validate you; you are already valuable and very peculiar. No two of you are in this world, and you have something useful to offer. Find yourself, love yourself, believe in yourself, and accept your true self." - Dr. Sandra C.Duru

Loving And Believing In Yourself Unleashes Your Potential - Stop Holding Back!

Hello, my darling. Are you aware that one of the enemy's biggest and most common tactics to destroy you is ensuring you fail to acknowledge, believe in, and love yourself? Yes, it is, and it sadly works to significant effect for him.

You have an unbelievable amount of greatness and potential stored in you by the Creator so that you can affect your generation and fulfill your purpose in life. Stop feeling inadequate because of your present situation, and never look to any man to validate or make you feel worthy, either.

No matter how things may look for you presently, I need you to know and understand that there are no two of you in this world, and you have something uniquely valuable to offer the world. However, you must find yourself, love, believe in yourself, and accept your true self to unleash and achieve your full potential.

Stop beating up and looking down on yourself, my dear. You are more than enough! There is so much untapped and hidden in you; your time of breaking forth and manifestation is now. The world awaits your glory. Arise, my kings and queens!

Day 113

"Always remember that the only real, true, and honest person you should try to be better than is that person you were yesterday. Prove yourself to yourself and not to others. You owe nobody any explanation for being who you are." - Dr. Sandra C. Duru

Your Only Competition Is You - There's Nothing To Prove!

My beloved darlings, how're you doing today? Do you know that we often put ourselves under unnecessary and avoidable pressure by trying to prove to others that we're worthy of their respect, attention, care, love, and all?

Please know today that the only standard you ever have to measure up to and become better than is the person you were yesterday. The Creator uniquely crafted and blessed you with abilities and a purpose tailored to suit all HE put in you. Stop competing or comparing yourself with anyone else!

Prove yourself to yourself and not to others. You owe nobody any explanation for being who you are because your race is as different from theirs as theirs is from yours.

Day 114

"Don't ever let the opinions of others interfere with this prevailing reality: It's your life, you are in charge of it, and you are not in competition with anyone." - Dr. Sandra C. Duru

It's Not Arrogance Or Pride - You're All That Matters!

Hello, my dear friend.

One vital thing I want you to have today is full assurance and confidence in the abilities, skills, talents, gifts, and vision the Creator has blessed you with. Your God-given purpose is not a public project but peculiar to you and all HE has deposited inside you.

Never allow anyone to run, rule over, or try to dictate or control how or what you can achieve. Don't be pressured into running against another person's clock either, because your destiny is unique, and you are not competing with anyone!

My dear, you must understand that you are all that matters and the only one who can decide whether you will fail or succeed. Knowing and walking in this truth is not pride or arrogance; you must never allow anyone to gaslight you into thinking or believing it is.

Day 115

"What you're capable of achieving is not a function of what other people think is possible for you or how they expect you to do it. What you're capable of achieving depends entirely on what you choose to do with your time, potential, resources, contacts, money, talent, intellectual abilities, skills, and energy." - Dr. Sandra C. Duru

Many Factors Determine Your Destiny In Life - People's Opinions Are Not Part Of Them.

My darlings, how are you today? I have been somehow pressed in my spirit to continue talking about this issue, and I believe it is because someone out there still needs to get and understand this truth deeply.

Many factors can either aid or destroy your destiny and God-given purpose in life. However, please be assured that other people's negative opinions, criticisms, projections, wishes, and bad words are not and can never be part of such factors!

Please know today that you are self-sufficient and much more than enough because this is what the Creator made you, and no one has the power to change or undermine it! Hence, you must also understand that your productivity and success depend entirely on what you choose to do with your time, potential, resources, contacts, money, talent, intellectual abilities, skills, and energy, and not on anyone else's opinions or words.

Day 116

"When you find yourself trapped between what moves you, what makes you feel fulfilled, and what society tells you is right for you, always travel the route that makes you feel alive, happy, and fulfilled – unless you want everyone to be happy, except you." - Dr. Sandra C. Duru

Always Look Out For Yourself At Any Crossroad - Your Happiness Matters!

My beloved darling, do you know that no one else is responsible for your joy, happiness, and fulfillment in this life but you?

Yes, you are the captain of this ship called your life, and you must never relinquish control and authority over it to anyone else. There are some exceptional moments when you may have to make selfless choices and decisions that suit others over yourself, but this should never become the norm.

Many people easily take good-natured and kindness for granted in others; hence you must always prioritize and look out for yourself at every crossroads in your life's journey. Your happiness matters greatly, and you must never allow anyone to tell you otherwise!

Day 117

"Always go for the things of greater value – the things money can't buy. What matters is having strength of character, an honest heart, a sense of self-worth, and credibility. Never sell if you're lucky enough to have any of these things. Never sell yourself short!" - Dr. Sandra C. Duru

Dignity And Credibility Are Vital - Money Is Not Everything!

Do you know that the roots of many of the problems we suffer worldwide can be traced to a few people's greed and lust to amass wealth at any cost?

My darling, nothing is more vital to you than your dignity, integrity, honor, good name, and faith. Never allow the quest and hunger for material things in this world to steal them from you. Never sell if you're lucky enough to have any of these things. Never sell yourself short!

No matter how much money you make in this life, no one will remember you by your bank balance once you're dead and gone but by your deeds and everything you stood for. Money is not everything, my dear; hence, you must always value and protect your credibility and dignity above all else.

Day 118

"Everyone wants to get to the top of the mountain first and shout, "Look at me! Look at me!" But the truth is, all your happiness, joy, abundance, and growth occur while you're climbing, not while you're sitting at the top." - Dr. Sandra C. Duru

Travails And Struggles Birth Growth - Stay The Course!

My beloved friends, are you aware you must do everything to ensure your craft is perfected and you're well grounded in your purpose before entering the limelight?

Many young people these days are too eager to "blow" and "become successful." However, they quickly forget one vital truth about life: Success is not about what you can achieve but what you can sustain, maintain, and recreate! Anyone can get to the top, but can you remain there?

Have you built and developed yourself well enough to last under the heat of leadership at the top? Don't be hungry for success prematurely because it is way more dangerous than the poverty you seek to escape. Go through your growth process and phase, and ensure you do not cut it short. It is for your good, my dear friend.

Day 119

"Walk your path confidently and don't expect anyone else to understand your life journey, especially if they have not been exactly where you are going or experienced what you have in life. You must take the bold steps right for you; no one else walks in your shoes." - Dr. Sandra C. Duru

Your Purpose Determines Your Path - Live And Love Your Unique Life.

Many things make us live and act the way we do, but our destinies are the most significant and influential factors. No two persons have the same, no matter how identical they may be!

Hence, my darling, you need to stop comparing yourself or the trajectory of your life to anyone else around you. You must devote yourself to discovering your God-given purpose in life and fully immerse yourself in it once you do. Oh, I cannot overstress the importance of this truth to you!

Your purpose determines your path in life, so you must learn to live and love your uniqueness daily. Walk your path confidently, my dear, and don't expect anyone else to understand your life journey - especially if they have not been exactly where you are going or experienced what you have in life.

Day 120

"Many times in life, we are the limitations and obstacles in our path by the thoughts we dwell on and the things we feed our spirit."
- Dr. Sandra C. Duru

What Do You Feed Your Spirit? Don't Be Your Greatest Hindrance!

My dear friends, how are you doing today? I'm pretty sure that you've heard many times that whatever a person's mind dwells on consistently is what they attract into their lives.

Well, I want to encourage you today to take this as seriously as possible because it is not just another of the numerous cliches flying around in the world. Yes, you can be the greatest hindrance to your God-given purpose, blessings, prosperity, and success if you only focus on negative thoughts, words, and actions instead of the goodness the Creator has surrounded you with.

What you feed your spirit is highly vital; hence, my constant and persistent harping on this issue of what you allow your mind to dwell on continually. You were created and born with a world of unlimited possibilities and absolutely no restrictions whatsoever.

Don't become the stumbling block and hindrance to your greatness by allowing negativity around and in your mind. Don't become a weapon against yourself and your own enemy!

Day 121

"The world needs that positive energy in you, but it cannot come forth if you keep living behind a prison wall of negative influence, thoughts, philosophies, doctrines, and mindsets that you feed yourself. You are better than this!" - Dr. Sandra C. Duru

Your Best Version Is Yet Dormant Within You - Unleash Your Potentials!

My love, I trust that your day has started well.

Do you know that the best version of you is yet hidden and laying dormant inside you because you are not feeding well enough to awaken the giant in you? No, my dear, this is not about carbohydrates and protein diets but about the mental stimulation, inspiration, motivation, and energy you feed to your spirit every minute through your thoughts and affirmations.

The Creator deposited something magnificent in you that the world craves, and nothing and no one is stopping you from manifesting and positively affecting generations and millions worldwide but yourself.

You are better and more highly gifted than those petty philosophies, human doctrines, and evil mindsets the enemy keeps trying to tie you down with, my dear. You are unstoppable!

However, you need to start feeding that limitless giant with the proper nutrients, or else your potential and greatness will remain dormant, and such would be a sad shame please.

Day 122

"Detoxify your mind and uncage yourself today. The world needs your unique ideas, visions, and potential. You were put on this planet for a reason, and it would be a huge shame to leave without fulfilling that purpose." - Dr. Sandra C. Duru

The Grave Is Filled With Unfulfilled Destinies - Don't Swell Its Ranks!

My beloved friend, how are you today? Has anyone ever told you that the wealthiest place on Earth is not Vatican City's gold reserves or any central bank in the world but the graveyards?

Graveyards are the wealthiest places on Earth because they hold an innumerable amount of unfulfilled destinies, potentials, God-given purposes, dreams, visions, goals, and an unquantifiable amount of riches that were never materialized.

Please, my dear, whatever you're going through today, make up your mind and strongly determine not to add to this already alarming number of people who live and pass away without fulfilling their purpose and missions on earth.

Such are those who swell the banks of the grave because they die without finishing their tasks and giving their all in their life's race. Inside you reside possibilities, abilities, and potentials that can change the world for good. Please don't leave this world without using them all!

Day 123

"When the time, place, and season are right, nobody and no demon can stop your blessings. Keep moving forward, and do not ever be in any competition with anyone. Whatever comes your way, thank God Almighty and remain strong." – Dr. Sandra C. Duru

Nothing Can Stop You When Your Time Is Right - Never Back Down!

Hello, my love. Do you know that when a person's time and season of restoration, deliverance, and breakthrough has arrived, they will be unstoppable in anything they do? Many will wonder why they seem so "lucky" in everything.

It is written that when God turns your captivity around, it will always feel like a dream to those watching around you. Hence, when it's your time to laugh, there is no power great enough in creation to stop you because the Maker of all things has approved your joy!

Never relent, back down, or be cowered by whatever obstacle you face today. Understand that your life's clock is different from every other person's, so it doesn't matter who is making it today or not because your time, too, will undoubtedly come! Let this be your motivation and driving force as you press on today, my dear, and always remember it.

Day 124

"If you ever find yourself at a point where you need to bow before money – which means to do something illegal, unethical, immoral, or against your principles to earn some quid – you need to call yourself to order." - Dr. Sandra C. Duru

The Worship Of Mammon Is Subtle - Resist It!

My beloved friend, how are you today? I'm sure you've heard severally that money itself is not evil, but the love of it is what makes it tainted. Now, do you know you may be worshipping it and unaware?

There are many slaves to the god of money called Mammon today that don't even know they're prisoners, while many know but couldn't care less. My love, if you ever have to compromise your faith, beliefs, virtue, and the truth, you know to earn anything, such money is Mammon supposedly, and you must resist it!

The blessings of God make you rich and add no sorrow to it. This is HIS word and truth; only through this can you find authentic, worthy, and lasting riches for yourself and future generations. Stand strong and firm for the truth always, no matter what sin and corruption offer, and in due time, you will surely be rewarded.

Day 125

"There are many things that you are capable of, and even more that you can achieve by simply being consistent. Am I referring only to your actions? No, I'm not, as the consistency required for you to become that successful icon you seek also involves your thoughts as much as your actions." - Dr. Sandra C. Duru

Your Actions Matter As Much As Your Thoughts - Watch Them!

Are you aware that besides your thoughts, your actions also have a very significant role to play in determining whether you will achieve your God-given purpose in life or not?

Hence, you must develop yourself and grow to the point where consistency becomes your trademark in all you do. Your thoughts shape your world and nature around you. However, you will achieve far more significant results once consistency becomes renowned, and your life and testimony will improve!

Day 126

"When you constantly feel worthless, devalued, unhappy, unappreciated, and unloved in a particular location, you may need to change that location immediately! Do not stay in such a place one second more before you get out of there fast!" - Dr. Sandra C. Duru

Get Away From People And Places Where You're Not Valued - You Deserve Better!

My love, how are you today? Have you ever considered that many of us would be living much better today if only we valued ourselves much better than we currently do?

Yes, my dear. Your life can be way better than it is presently if you refuse to allow anyone to look down on or maltreat you in any way. More so, the signs are always there for you to see, yet you ignore them and wonder why no one seems to value you.

Please get away from anyone and anywhere you know you're not genuinely loved, appreciated, and valued because you deserve way better than such in life, my love!

Day 127

"Every one of us was created to add value to this earth in one way or the other, so there is no human being in the world that is useless and without value." - Dr. Sandra C. Duru

Everything God Created Is Precious - You Are Not An Exception!

Hello love. How has your day started today? I have a short word from the maker of nature itself, and it gives me pleasure to share because it's one of my favorite passages.

"And God saw every thing that he had made, and, behold, it was very good. And the evening and the morning were the sixth day." - Genesis 1:31. The Maker of all things looked at everything, including you, and said it is "very good."

My dear, for no reason must you ever allow anyone to belittle or talk down at you again because you are a jewel of inestimable value! Your glory may not have been revealed yet, but make no mistake that it will, and your relevance will be celebrated in this world and the one to come as long as you never relent or quit on yourself!

Day 128

"Your dreams, goals, and vision may get you into trouble or even a challenging situation, but never mind. You will be fine if you hold on to God and never give up on them." - Dr. Sandra C. Duru

Never Mind Troubles If They Come Because Of Your Dreams - You Are Doing Well!

My love, are you aware that your dreams, visions, ambitions, desires, and purpose can often land you into severe trouble? How should you now deal with such situations? Let me remind you about someone today.

The little boy Joseph, son of Jacob, was divinely gifted with the gift of dreams, their interpretation, and wisdom. However, these gifts seemed to land him in grave danger as his brothers were very jealous of him and eventually plotted to kill him initially before selling him off into slavery instead.

Was it easy for him to suffer and endure all these? No, not at all, but he stayed faithful and held on to his Maker's vision. Eventually, the gifts and dreams God gave him made way for him out of prison and slavery, and he could fulfill his purpose.

You are doing just fine, my dear, but please, don't mind any trouble arising against you because of your peculiar and unique dream. One day soon, it will all be worth it!

Day 129

"There's a purpose and a unique reason for your existence. What you are going through at the moment is not in any way to destroy you. Instead, it is to equip you for a better future. Learn from it, build strength, persevere, and don't give up." - Dr. Sandra C.Duru

That Storm Is To Build, Not Destroy You - Learn From It!

Has anyone ever told you that every storm and trial God allows to come your way is not to destroy but to build, toughen, strengthen, and equip you for the purpose HE created you for?

Learn from your trials, afflictions, and tribulations, and never allow anything or anyone to make you feel worthless or forsaken because of them. Your Maker has promised never to allow any temptation beyond your power to come your way, remember?

Hence, no matter the situation, always look for the lessons in every ordeal and make the most of them. God's got you covered, so why would you continue to fret over anything, my love?

Day 130

"Your life, future, businesses, career, lovely children, and safety are in God's hands and not in the hands of any man. Keep shining!" - Dr. Sandra C. Duru

God Is Your Assured Security - Why Worry About Anything?

There's one passage in the good book I love so much, and it's somewhere in the book of the Prophets. It assures the goodness that comes from trusting in God, no matter what you face.

"Thou wilt keep him in perfect peace, whose mind is stayed on thee: because he trusteth in thee." - Isaiah 26:3. My dear, the key to your security and peace in life are in your hands; that much you can see and understand by these words.

Never surrender them to the enemy by dwelling on negativity and endless worries. The Maker of everything is your assured security, so why worry about anything, my love? Is there anything, any power, and anyone greater than HE?

Fear not, and keep shining. You are destined for greatness in life, and nothing shall stop you from living and achieving your purpose!

Day 131

"Do you know that the bigger your dreams and visions, the harder the enemy will fight against you, and the more obstacles and trials you will have to overcome on your path? Don't cave in, and never be discouraged!" - Dr. Sandra C. Duru

The Size Of Your Destiny Determines Your Level Of Opposition - Never Cave In!

My love, do you know that the amount of energy you will expend trying to My love, do you know that the amount of energy you will expend trying to pick up a piece of paper on the ground is not close to that you will need to lift a 10kg dumbbell?

This is an exact analogy of how your destined glory and God-given purpose determine the level and intensity of the opposition you will encounter while trying to break through and achieve your purpose. The bigger your destiny and dreams, the more challenging and stronger the opposition and battles you must face and win to get to it.

Brace yourself, my champion! There's still a battle at every corner, but be not dismayed or discouraged because you already have all it takes to come out victorious always!

Day 132

"It does not matter how slowly you go as long as you do not stop. Never give up; that is where and when the tide will turn. You just can't beat the person who won't give up. There is no failure except in no longer trying." - Dr. Sandra C. Duru

Your Speed Doesn't Matter. Your Movement Does. Never Stop!

Hello, my love. Have you ever wondered the wise voice of nature says that a living dog is better than a dead lion? I'll give you a simple illustration to help you better understand this today.

No matter how ferocious a lion's statue looks, a living and well-fed Rottweiler will better protect you anytime. This also applies to your movement and progress in life, my dear. Please stop waiting for that "big push" or that "banging break" before you move!

No matter how gifted or talented you are, if you don't try to perfect your craft and showcase it to the world, you will only exist and eventually exit this world with zero achievements. This should and will never be your story.

So, my dear, whatever it takes, keep moving. Slow movement is forever better than no movement. And, if you keep it up, no matter how slow it may seem, you will surely get to your point of excellent glory sooner than later.

Day 133

"While giving up when the going gets tough might sound tempting, learning to persevere and finish strong is much more rewarding. You must often ignore what people say and remain focused." -Dr. Sandra C. Duru

Protect Your Focus Always - It's Invaluable!

My beloved friend, how has the going been for you lately? Do you struggle to keep pushing toward your desired and destined mark because of all the trials and challenges that never seem to stop?

I want you to know today that the enemy keeps bombarding you like that because he wants you to lose focus and become distracted by keeping your eyes on the troubles instead of the crown ahead of you.

Your focus is invaluable, my dear friend; you must do everything possible to protect it! Let the storms and all those tongues continue to rage against you. As long as you don't throw in the towel, you will stand tall in triumph over them all eventually, and all you're enduring now will be worth it in the long run. Stay strong!

Day 134

"Bad words can build some people and make them fruitful and better than their attackers and bullies in the near future. The same bad words can ruin the lives of others completely. It all depends on you." - Dr. Sandra C. Duru

What They Say Doesn't Matter - How You Take It Does.

My love, do you know that nobody in creation has the power to ruin you with their words or even actions if you don't permit them to? Yes, the enemy is powerless against you if you stand your ground!

The good book admonishes us to guard our hearts with all diligence - it is because of issues like these, my dear. What you do with all the hate, bile, jealousy, and vicious words the enemy hurls at you is within your control, and you can choose to let them be fuel for your passion instead of the ammunition for your destruction.

The choice is entirely yours, my love.

Day 135

"Don't ever allow anyone to mess with your mind. If your mental health is messed up, you are completely ruined." - Dr. Sandra C. Duru

Your Mind Is The Gateway To All You Are - Guard It Well!

Have you ever wondered why kings and generals in medieval times always liked to lay siege against an enemy's location and spread their vast armies in plain sight for them to see?

It's because wars and battles are first fought and won in the mind before any physical combat begins. Anyone who successfully defeats or subdues you mentally has already won any other battle against you.

Hence, you must be wary of those you grant access to your mind because if one tiny weed is planted there, your entire vineyard will eventually be laid to waste by it if you don't act fast and pull it out!

Everything you will become depends on how healthy your mind is. Please guard it well consistently.

Day 136

"Wherever you find yourself, there's a good reason, and you're needed there. There's something good waiting for you there. Don't forget that nothing good comes so very easily. But when you eventually break through, you will never remain the same. Genuine success comes in stages and phases." - Dr. Sandra C. Duru

Good Success Never Comes All At Once - Be Calm.

Do you know there is no excellent or lasting success without a trail of hard-fought victories and tales of tedious exploits?

Anything short of this, my dear, is like expecting a seed to spring out from the soil and start bearing fruits the same week you plant it. Success takes time to build and achieve, my beloved. Please don't be in a hurry.

The glory and success you crave will come, but you must go through this grueling process now so that your victory and joy can be an enduring one later.

Day 137

"Nobody is useless. Stop stressing or worrying about your educational qualifications, background, or what people will say. Instead, focus more on your life and how to earn a sustainable income to better it." - Dr. Sandra C. Duru

Everyone Has Something To Offer - Nobody Is Useless!

If there is one beautiful thing that I have discovered and come to love so much about nature, it is that no leaves, roots, or plant is useless on this earth. That you're ignorant of their uses doesn't mean they are worthless.

The question now is: If the Creator could be so purposeful about plants and leaves, how much more you made in HIS image and likeness? Whatever you do, don't ever allow anyone to tell or make you feel worthless and useless!

If that plant is not without a purpose, then you certainly have so much more deposited inside you, my dear. Find it, hone it to perfection, and you will begin to prosper and affect your world with it.

Day 138

"You have the potential to be very great and successful. Stop complaining and start taking possession today. It doesn't matter if you must start life from scratch. I started life from scratch in a foreign country, and today, I am a living testimony. You can do it!" - Dr. Sandra C. Duru

Complaints Don't Take You Anywhere - Take Action Instead!

My love, can I ask you a question today? If you are in a hurry to a destination but get stuck in a terrible traffic jam along your commute, will you remain in the same spot and complain when the traffic eases eventually, or will you continue driving?

I bet you would continue driving and keep pushing to your destination, wouldn't you? This applies to our daily lives and activities, though, and sadly, many of us fail at it badly. When faced with unpleasant situations, we often stay in the same spot and whine about it for too long instead of letting go and moving on with our lives.

Don't make that mistake anymore today. Whatever obstacles stand in your way, don't stay and complain about them. Instead, take action by running through them if you have to, and by all means, keep moving!

Day 139

"Stand mighty against all storms and pain. They are nothing but a dim-lit pathway to your shining heroic destiny. The storms that come your way are tools for shaping and strengthening, not occasions to break or destroy you." - Dr. Sandra C. Duru

Let Your Storms Define You...Not Destroy You!

Hello, my love. Have you observed one apparent similarity between life and our educational systems? It is how pupils are graded and promoted after thorough exams.

Life's exams, tests, and continuous assessments are the storms, trials, pains, and tribulations it keeps bringing your way. And, like the school exams you've been writing, these are only to certify your fitness and ability to handle the glory and promotions ahead. They are never to destroy you!

So, please, begin to see them as what they are from today; let the storms of life define and not destroy you, and you will surely excel and overcome as you do.

Day 140

"What obstacles kept you from your vision yesterday? Make them your stepping stone today! Get it done and move to the next. No matter the challenges and distractions, great achievers with their eyes set on their goals don't lose focus." - Dr. Sandra C. Duru

No Power Can Keep You Down If You Dont Want To - It's Your Call.

Do you know that one thing life guarantees us is that there will always be obstacles, trials, hurdles, tribulations, and battles to scale through? Hence, you must neither rest in yesterday's victories nor wallow in self-pity over today's defeat.

Turn your obstacles and the giants before you into stepping stones by being absolutely resilient, and never take no for an answer! Those who move and work like this are always focused on their end goals; hence, they never lose!

You can be more and do more with your dreams, vision, goals, and God-given purpose, too, if only you would refuse to stay down and keep pushing till your breakthrough manifests. The choice is truly yours, my dear. Please make the right call.

Day 141

"Know when to throw some distractions in the garbage. Know when to use them as manure to grow your planted seeds of success. Know when to crush and recycle them to your best use, and also know when to get them taken away from you completely by dealing with them as you deem fit and necessary." - Dr. Sandra C. Duru

Distractions Can Be Useful...If You Know How To Utilize Them!

I'm sure you're wondering if that header is a mistake on my part, but it is not, my love. Yes, distractions and any other spanner the enemy throws into your work can become valuable tools.

However, the trick is knowing how to use them to your advantage so that the very thing the enemy intended to destroy you with becomes a stepping stone to your greatness!

And, if you're still wondering if this is even possible at all, do you remember the story and life of Judas Iscariot? The enemy thought he was supposedly the ultimate stumbling block in the ministry of Jesus on earth, but the Master turned him into one the most vital tools to accomplish HIS purpose.

There is something valuable in everything around you. God wouldn't have let them enter your space if there weren't. So, instead of seeing only distractions and obstacles when encountering them, begin to see bountiful opportunities and possibilities in everything, and you will be amazed at what you can achieve.

Day 142

"What's done is done. What's gone is gone. One of life's lessons is always moving on. It's okay to look back to see how far you've come, but always keep moving forward." - Dr. Sandra C. Duru

Your Rearview Mirror Is For Acceleration - Don't Let It Slow You Down.

My beloved friend, how are you today? Do you know that the purpose of that rearview mirror on your vehicle and motorbike is to let you know when and how to accelerate and not stop?

No one actively racing on the track looks into their rearview to slow down but to see who may be catching up with them so that they can speed up and get to the finish line first. Your past and memories from it are your rearview mirror, my dear.

Please stop letting it slow you down or even stop you dead in your tracks because you've refused to take your eyes off it. Whatever is in your past is behind you already, so you must keep moving and never let it slow you down or stop you again.

Day 143

"Don't ever think of giving up in life. It's not bad to create boundaries when needed. Again, do not be available for everyone and everything; instead, be valuable!" – Dr. Sandra C. Duru

Wisdom Says To Be Valuable But Not Available For Everything - Here's Why!

Have you ever considered that many gifted and talented people have given up on life and stopped pursuing their divine purposes because they failed to set healthy boundaries around themselves?

Yes, it is good to be kind and selfless to others, but it is foolishness ever to allow anyone else to dictate, rule, or control how your time and life should be spent, no matter who they are!

My love, learn to create healthy boundaries even while you selflessly help others. By so doing, everyone around you will know that you are indeed valuable but not always available for anything detrimental or of no essence to your dreams, goals, ambitions, and purpose in life. This is the voice of nature and wisdom, my dear. Be wise!

Day 144

"Do more, achieve more, be more, and show less. By so doing, the enemies of progress around you will not know what to attack." – Dr. Sandra C. Duru

There Is Safety In Silence - Be Discreet!

My love, I trust that you are doing great today. There is a passage in the good book that I've always pondered upon and have also come to love so much since I came upon it.

The wisest man and king to ever live said: "Even a fool, when he holdeth his peace, is counted wise: And he that shutteth his lips is esteemed a man of understanding." - Proverbs 17:28. Wise people always dwell in safety all their days because they never give away anything the enemy can demonize against them at any point in time.

There is much safety in silence and being discreet, my beloved. Stop announcing your every achievement and plan to the world. Learn to be secretive and discreet; you will surely be more and do more in life, my dear.

Day 145

"Pay no attention to distractions, detractors, and toxic people. Your achievements are not for a show-off or to compete with anyone in and out of social media but for you to feel fulfilled and enjoy your beautiful life silently." – Dr. Sandra C. Duru

Social Media Is Not For Showoff - Enjoy Your Life Quietly!

Are you aware that soldiers wear camouflage because they easily blend in with their surroundings during combat and do not attract attention to themselves?

Sadly, one of the most significant harms we do ourselves is our inexplicable penchant for competing and showing off, which is very much against the ways of nature and who we're meant to be. My love, please don't be sucked in and ruined by this kind of lifestyle where everything about your life is always out there on social media!

You are not competing with anyone; anything you do and achieve must not be announced and displayed to the world. Keep your success and life discreet, and you will have fewer battles to fight. Ignore those evil naysayers and mockers and enjoy your life quietly, my love.

Day 146

"Don't let ordinary circumstances dim the shine of the extraordinary you. Stand mighty against all storms and pain. They are nothing but a dim-lit pathway to your shining heroic destiny." - Dr. Sandra C. Duru

Fire And Pressure Reveal Things - What Are You Made Of?

My beloved friend, how are you doing today? Do you know that fire and extreme heat are more purifiers than destroyers, depending on what you place in them? Walk to a goldsmith's workplace, and you'll learn much, my dear.

When heavy pressure is mounted on you, and the heat of life blazes hard against you, what do you become? Do you crack, become discouraged and depressed, and throw in the towel? Or do you buckle up and begin to shine through such fiery storms?

Never allow any situation to drag you down permanently because you are much greater than any obstacle confronting you. Your glorious destiny awaits, my dear, and these flames are your preparation for the glory ahead. Endure them and never be found wanting!

Day 147

"The most important factor distinguishing you from everyone anywhere you go is your cultural values, uniqueness, and beliefs. Once this is eroded or lost, you are no different from everyone around you, and the unique edge for you to become and remain outstanding is sadly lost." - Dr. Sandra C. Duru

The Can Be No Fake Without An Original - Never Lose Yourself!

My love, has anyone ever told you that to have a fake or adulterated thing or product, there must first be an original of it?

There can never be a fake without an original; hence, you must always be on your guard not to become something and someone you're not by copying anything around you! The Creator made us special and gifted us with unique abilities and qualities to establish and secure our divine purposes.

Why hop on trends that keep changing around you and lose your uniqueness, trying to be a copy of what someone else is when God has put so much in you to be original, too? Don't you know that you can create your unique trend too and have others follow it if they want to instead of you becoming a copy of them?

Come on, my dear! You can do and also deserve much better than a fake life of copying others. So, please, don't ever lose yourself this way.

Day 148

> "It's imperative to recognize, accept, and honor your unique culture and heritage, and never forget your roots. Our cultural heritage is our pride, joy, strength, honor, and uniqueness." - Dr. Sandra C. Duru

Your Culture And Roots Are Invaluable - Cherish Them!

There is a famous saying in Africa that any river that forgets its source will eventually dry off, and this harsh truth of nature applies to you as a person, too, my love.

God deliberately made and gave us our different cultural heritages, traditions, customs, and roots as our unique identifiers and for guidance in whatever part of the world we find ourselves in.

Refusing to accept and honor your roots means that you're choosing to forget where you come from and who you originally were, and if you continue on such a path, you will sadly end up like that river. A person who doesn't know where they're coming from can never know where they're truly meant to be.

This is the sad plight of anyone who forgets or chooses to ignore their roots. Please don't end up like that, my beloved friend.

Day 149

"There's no reason to remain where you're unhappy, victimized, maltreated, unappreciated, and constantly used. Leave now, and watch your peace and happiness blossom, even as you flourish." - Dr. Sandra C. Duru

Your Peace And Happiness Are In Your Hands - Secure Them!

My dear, do you know you have the power and right to determine how happy, peaceful, and well your life can be, no matter the situation and conditions around you, at any time?

Yes, you can, and this is why I consistently tell everyone around me this truth: Part of the reason why the Creator gave you legs is so you can walk away from anything that's a constant threat to your joy and mental well-being!

Why would you choose to remain with people and in places where all you get is toxic narcissism, needless hatred, and constant wickedness? Again, I tell you, my love, you are worth so much more and certainly deserve better in life than that, so please secure your happiness by walking away today!

Day 150

"We were all made to make positive and lasting impacts in the lives of everyone God allows to cross our paths. Hence, we must live purposeful and intentional lives so that we will be able to achieve this purpose." - Dr. Sandra C. Duru

Never Live For Yourself Alone - You Were Made For More!

Have you ever been told there is more to your existence than your personal life and achievements because so many other destinies are linked to yours?

The great Apostle Paul once said that the creation eagerly awaits the manifestations of the sons of God because many people and even things in nature may not prosper and become what they're meant to be if you do not do well. Please keep this truth in mind and remember it always!

You were created to make a remarkable impact in people's lives as they cross your path in life, but you must first prepare yourself to be able to do so. How can you give to others when you're empty, and how won't you become empty if you don't live a purposeful, disciplined, deliberate, and very intentional life?

You were created for more than just yourself, my love, so you must begin to seek to be more and do more with your life daily!

Day 151

"If there is one thing that virtually everyone in this world always makes the mistake of thinking we have in abundance, it is time. Sadly, though, this is the one so-called 'gift' of nature that none of us has because it waits for nobody!" - Dr. Sandra C. Duru

Stop Being Deluded - Time Is Not Your Friend!

My dear friend, sometimes the best love we can get from those who care about us is a good version of tough love, hence the tone of my short headline above.

In all you do today, I need you to know this fact and keep it within you always: Time is nobody's friend, so you must stop wasting it! There's a reason why wise men of old said, "Tick says the clock...what you have to do, do quickly," remember?

Stop thinking you can recover whatever time you waste on frivolities; don't even engage in such behavior to begin with! Learn to manage your time efficiently, and all your dreams, hopes, plans, visions, ambitions, and aspirations will be perfect.

Day 152

"The older you get, the longer and thicker the shadows of the past become. But what's important here is not holding on to them. You cannot turn the clock back, but you can do your best today to make tomorrow happier." - Dr. Sandra C. Duru

Yesterday's Gone Already, But You Have Power Over Today And Tomorrow.

I have seen a great evil under the sun, and it gets even worse by the day because it's almost as though each new generation is pre-programmed to continue in this error of those before them.

My love, please don't get caught up in a life that refuses to leave what's gone behind and focus on the immensely limitless possibilities the present has to offer - today is called the "present" for a reason, you know?

No matter the situation, please understand that yesterday is gone already, and you can do nothing about it. However, you have every power and control over what you can achieve today, and you can become tomorrow, too.

So, please don't waste it by dwelling on the past. No one goes forward or makes any progress in life by constantly looking behind them, remember?

Day 153

"Always remember that everything you need to succeed is within you, and they are on your pathway. You will not discover or even find them until you start walking on your path." – Dr. Sandra C. Duru

Walking In Your Path Is Key To Your Success - Stop Living A Lie!

My beloved, do you know that anything you do outside that which the Creator has predestinated you for is a waste of your time and HIS precious resources, and you should never engage in such?

Trying to be like someone else or taking a path because your friend did the same and it paid off is a subtle trap of the enemy to lure you away from where and what you should be. I remember how many young children I knew back in high school who went off to college to study courses they had zero passion for because their friends were doing it. Today, many have realized their grave error, but sadly, it has cost them years they cannot regain.

Walk in your path, my dear, and stay on it no matter how hard or long it seems to be. You have a unique destiny, and your journey must always reflect this truth. All you need to succeed has been deposited inside you already. Stay true to yourself, and you will undoubtedly achieve that desired greatness in due time!

Day 154

"There are some things in life that no one else can do for you because they have been programmed to happen as you take the needed steps and actions to actualize them daily. Get moving today!" – Dr. Sandra C. Duru

Everything You Need Will Happen For You - Don't Worry!

Hello, my love. I know that many times in life, it seems like we are reaching for straws while pursuing our dreams, goals, visions, and God-given purpose.

I would have you know, though, that this is certainly not true because your Maker is not an irresponsible Father who would ever do such to you! All you need to accomplish everything you desire has been provided, even before birth.

However, at each point and phase of your life, there are specific actions you will be required to take before you can get these provisions. A man who doesn't leave his bedroom when others go out early to cultivate their farms and plant should not expect a harvest when those who worked enjoy theirs.

This is the simple rule of life, and those who obey and walk in it will always enjoy it to the fullest. Get moving today, my dear, and you, too, will enjoy all you have been destined to have in life.

Day 155

"If If you want to start seeing those dreams and visions come to fruition, you must learn to step into your powers to start living your dream! Step into your blessings, and live your purpose without apologies, regrets, or fears." – Dr. Sandra C. Duru

Step Into Your Powers And Live Without Apologies - You Owe No One!

Have you ever been told that the power to actualize and achieve all your dreams, goals, and God-given purpose in life has already been given to you, but you may never live up to your potential if you keep living a timid and subdued life?

Step into your powers by embracing your true identity and live without apologizing to anyone, my dear! Those who have ruled and dominated every sphere they've stepped into in the history of humanity have been fearless enough to never cower before anyone or obstacles in pursuing their dreams!

You have been given all you need to prosper and flourish, but you must begin to take charge and live true to your calling lest you fall short and shortchange yourself eventually.

Live boldly, fearlessly, and free, my love and the world will be the canvas your glory will be painted, too.

Day 156

"The gifting and blessings of God in your life are not for you to be hidden in a corner or to live an oppressed, unfilled, and timid life on earth. A lion does not give birth to goats, and no child of a king can be born into slavery or as an insecure person, ever!" – Dr. Sandra C. Duru

God Did Not Create You To Be A Slave To Anything - Stop Living Like One!

My dear, do you know that, by every right and even the laws that be, no child of a king or ruler can ever be raised as an enslaved person in the same palace their parents are?

Well, are you also aware that when you allow yourself to live an oppressed, tormented, and subdued life without fighting to break free from such afflictions, you are like that royal child being treated like a slave in the palace where they should be ruling?

Please, don't ever allow anything or anyone to subdue and torment your life in any way, my dear! You are the child of the King of all kings, and HE did not create and endue you with all HE has for you to be hidden and dominated in life.

You are highly blessed, favored, and gifted, my love. It's high time you start living as such!

Day 157

"You are not God, and you don't have the powers to add or subtract the number of years you'll have to exist on earth. You don't want to waste more time on complaints and frivolities, do you?" – Dr. Sandra C. Duru

No one Knows Their Appointed Time On Earth - Stop Wasting Yours!

The issue of life, death, and the great beyond has been an interesting topic for many ages, but there is something I find even more intriguing.

It is a fact that while engrossed in so many trivial and meaningless things, many people never seem to remember that none of us can live forever, and time is never on anyone's side! So today, I want to encourage you, my dear, to please stop living like you hold the controls of life and time in your hands - no created being does!

Live daily as if it would be your last, and pursue your dreams, goals, and purpose like you wouldn't be here tomorrow. You will be pleasantly amazed at the incredible levels of success you will begin to stressless walk and operate in consistently.

No one knows their appointed time on earth. Please stop wasting yours, my beloved.

Day 158

"Everyone wants to be successful and move forward to the next level, but every new level is a great challenge. You must be well prepared to persevere and be determined to succeed." – Dr. Sandra C. Duru

Success Has A Price - Can You Pay It?

My love, I'm pretty confident that if we were to take a public poll right now and ask people about the kind of life they would like to live if everything were free, nobody would ever choose to be poor or live an average life!

However, everything in life has well-laid rules and ordinances they follow and answer to, and success is no different. To be all you dream and pray to be, you must be willing to put in the required work and effort and make sacrifices at each phase of your journey.

Then and only then can you have that kind of life you crave, and this time, it will be sweet, lasting, and enduring because you paid the due price and earned it! Success has a price, my darling. Are you willing to go the extra mile and pay for it?

Voice Of Nature (Vol.1) By Sandra Duru

Day 159

"You must be an all-weather fan of nature to succeed in life. It's like what I always tell my children: Success has no season; you have to be an all-season person to be very successful in life." – Dr. Sandra C. Duru

There Is No Allotted Time For Success - It Can Happen To You At Any Time!

Hello, my love. Do you know that, unlike rain, snow, harmattan, and other seasonal natural phenomena, success has no time or season in a year allotted to it, and it can happen to anyone at any time?

Yes, my dear! Every day is a day to be blessed, fruitful, and excel at anything you do because the only thing success answers to is preparation and opportunity. Hence there must never be a time or period in life when you're not prepared to take any opportunity nature, and your Creator pushes your way!

The breakthrough and success you so earnestly crave can come to you anytime because there is no allotted time for them on the calendar. The question is: Will you be ready?

Day 160

"Great people do not focus so much on the negatives that they forget the positives. Great people are all-season, all-weather, and all-time achievers. They can work anywhere, anytime, and always ready to go get things done correctly without being sluggish." – Dr. Sandra C. Duru

There's A Reason Why Great People Rarely Miss - Here's Why!

My beloved, I want to ask you an interesting question today.

If two people were to be called upon to contest in a race, what would the outcome be if one of them prepares and trains well while the other person only goes around complaining about the terms of the race instead of training too?

I'm sure your guess is as good as mine on this, too - the latter will be defeated heavily because his focus was on the wrong things before and during the race. Sadly, this is how many of us live our daily lives today, yet we keep hoping for different results.

Life is not magic, my dear. Great people hardly fail or miss in life because they're laser-focused and don't waste time on irrelevant things that have nothing positive to contribute to their purpose.

If you want to start seeing this type of result in your life, you must be willing to learn from them and focus more on the tasks ahead of you rather than the obstacles, challenges, and negatives around your goals.

You can and will be celebrated, too, but you must learn to live right always. There are no shortcuts!

Day 161

"Your success may be trapped in your weaknesses. Work on your weaknesses, un-trap, and free yourself. We were all created to be uniquely great and successful." – Dr. Sandra C. Duru

You May Be Your Biggest Enemy Yet - Conquer Yourself!

My dear, one of the oldest tricks the enemy has used to attack and destroy people over the ages is to find their weaknesses and weaponize them against them. Sadly, it always has, and is still working to devastating effect.

Are you aware that you may be your biggest enemy, especially if you continue to live a reckless, frivolous, and indisciplined lifestyle? Be wary of your vices and those you love to indulge in, my dear. You're not the only one who knows about them, as the enemy has been watching and is always plotting and scheming to bring you down.

You were created and fully equipped to do and achieve great things in life, my dear. Don't be your nemesis by how you live, especially the so-called pleasures you constantly indulge in!

Day 162

"When you are financially blessed and stable, it's not for a show! It's for you to live well, live right, be very comfortable, and carry out your purpose here on earth, and nothing more." – Dr. Sandra C. Duru

Your Wealth And Blessings Are Not To Oppress Others - Don't Be Foolish!

When listing the greatest evils he had seen under the sun, the wisest king and man who lived said that one was for a beggar to be seated in a place of wealth and honor (paraphrased).

Does this mean he doesn't want poor people to become rich and have better lives? No, it doesn't. The poverty King Solomon refers to here is that of the mind, which is far worse and more significant than the emptiness you see in your wallet or bank account.

See, wealth and riches in the hands of a poor person will make them misbehave and act foolishly because their hands have touched way more than their minds can handle! Don't ever be such a person, my dear.

Your wealth and blessings are not to oppress others but to lift and show God's goodness to them. And, you are given every resource you get in life so that your God-given purpose may be fulfilled. Please don't be foolish!!

Day 163

"Fake lifestyle will only make your life more miserable. Find your true self, develop your potential, and your life will turn around for good." – Dr. Sandra C. Duru

Your Joy Lies In Staying True To Yourself - It Is Up To You.

My love, I have a short word from nature for you today, and I would love for you to pay rapt attention to it. Are you aware that the faster you run away from being fake, the quicker your blessings and success will manifest?

A famous joke in Africa talks about how angels may miss some people they're sent to because those people have changed everything about their lives into what they are not and are living fake lives. While many laughed and still laugh when this is told, I've always pondered deeply on the hidden truths inside the humor.

Don't rob and deny yourself the goodness you're supposed to effortlessly gain from your Creator, nature, and everything around you if you stay true to yourself.

Your fulfillment and joy depend on how well you can stay true to and develop yourself. This is nature's undisputed truth, and it's all up to you, my beloved.

Day 164

"The best thing you can do is follow your heart, work hard, remain focused, be honest to yourself, prayerful, determined, and brave. In trying not to make mistakes in life, many people have made far graver errors in places where there can be no remedy for such failings." – Dr. Sandra C. Duru

Running From Mistakes Will Lead You To More - Face And Embrace Them!

Do you remember the story of another great king who once lived and achieved tremendous things in his lifetime, but his testimony was almost destroyed by one mistake he made and tried to cover up?

King David made the mistake of resting at home when other kings were at war. Then he added the error of gazing at another man's wife lustfully, forcing her into his bed, and then crowning it with the gravest mistake of killing her husband to cover up his act of impregnating her during his act of infidelity.

The consequences of his actions were dire and even fatal for his children, and I would like you to learn from this, my dear. Please stop trying to cover up mistakes when you make them, especially those you may be unable to avoid.
Your actions may lead to graver errors, which may be much worse than what you're trying to cover up. So, please, don't be so terrified of making mistakes that you now commit worse blunders. Face and embrace them whenever you do, and don't be forced into bigger ones because of fear!
Let God guide your ways and path always, and I assure you that you will turn out perfectly well in the long run.

Day 165

"Your life may not be perfect, but you are alive and will get it right. The road may be slippery, rough, stormy, and full of thorns, but you will find the right path to safety, peace, love, and freedom if only you remain strong, true to yourself, and faithful to God." – Dr. Sandra C. Duru

You Are Still Alive And Well - That's All That Matters!

My love, you may recall that I've spoken this famous scripture to you during one of our earlier chats, but it's also quite relevant right now, if not even more so.

"A living dog is better than a dead lion," said the wise man, whose words could not be more valid today. See, no matter what you're facing and battling with presently; you must never forget that you still have the most significant gift anything and anyone in creation could ever have: your life!

Even if you're struggling with some severe health challenges right now, do you know that you can even feel that pain because you're still alive, and while you yet do, you are indeed not hopeless?

Stay strong and true to yourself, my darling. No matter what the battles, trials, tribulations, challenges, obstacles, and situations are, you are still alive and well enough to read or even hear this, and that is all that matters! As long as you remain alive, it's only a matter of time. Your testimonies, too, will break forth, and many shall rejoice with you if you do not give up.

Day 166

"Do not let the memories of your past limit your future potential. There are no limits to what you can achieve on your journey through life, except in your mind." – Dr. Sandra C. Duru

The Only Limit You Have Is Your Mind - Train It Well.

Hello, my beloved. Are you aware that, like every other muscle in your body, your mind can also be trained to withstand, endure, and carry any amount and level of weight, stress, and pain?

Yes, you can, and the voice of nature to you today urges you to do just that - train your mind and break every known limits and bounds you've ever encountered because there are indeed no limits to all you can achieve!

However, if you allow such a potent force like your mind to lie fallow, undeveloped, and untrained, you will reap the fruits of such inaction, but I bet they won't be pleasant results. The only limit your life has is your mind, my love. Please train it well!

Day 167

"Growth never stops. With a life full of possibilities, you have the potential to keep building on your progress and laying the foundation for your best self. Even if you've already achieved some of your goals, you can always do more and be better." – Dr. Sandra C. Duru

There Is Always More To Achieve And Conquer - Stay Hungry!

I recently heard that a famous football team in a top European league won and dominated that country for ten straight years, and I couldn't help but smile to myself.

That team affirms something that nature desires to teach you today, my love, and it is that no matter how much you attain and achieve today, yesterday's victories are gone with it, and they can never be enough.

While your exploits from yesterday may earn you respect, they can never earn you the crown or titles today because they no longer count! There is always more ground to break and new territories and achievements to conquer, so you must always stay hungry for more, my dear.

This is the hallmark and logo of champions and world-beaters, and you, my darling, must be identified as one, too, in life.

Day 168

"Take risks. Don't always take the safe and easy route because you're afraid of what might happen or what people will say about you. Let them say, let them condemn you at first, but later you will watch them imitate you and your style." – Dr. Sandra C. Duru

Those Who Judge You Today Will Celebrate You Tomorrow - Never Relent!

My dear friend, one of the many things that have always fascinated me about the human character is how many people switch their opinions and allegiances depending on current situations and achievements.

Please, if this is all you learn today, know that it is well worth it, and you must guard it jealously and use it well. Never live your life based on what people will say about you, and you must surely never quit or fail to pursue opportunities out of fear of what others will think and say about you!

Fortune and history only favor and remember the brave and victorious ones, so you must never relent. All who oppose and abuse you today will be the first to kowtow before you when you succeed tomorrow.

Let this truth be your driving force and inspiration, and you will achieve unimaginable things, my dear.

Day 169

"To build great potential, you must be very focused and determined to make it happen without doubts or fears. Kill that fear in you, and watch yourself live up to your infinite potential." – Dr. Sandra C. Duru

Nothing Grows In An Environment Of Fear - Get Rid Of It!

Hello, my dear. Have you ever seen any farmer plant some grain of corn, then when he notices that it has sprouted from the soil, he covers it with a metal bucket, doesn't ever water it again, yet expects it to grow and yield many ears of corn?

As absurd as this may sound, this is precisely what you do to yourself whenever you allow doubts and fear to cripple your mind to the point where you struggle to think and function properly anymore.

Fear is a toxic parasite that destroys anything it latches on to because it is never associated with goodness. Nothing good can ever grow in an environment of fear, doubt, and uncertainty.

Get rid of them, and you're on your way to a life of flourishing, freedom, and rest. Oh, and please...start today!

Day 170

"Bad weather doesn't last forever. The wet, rainy, icy, slippery roads will dry up. The storms will calm down. The dried-up trees and leaves will flourish again. And there will be a new season. Only believe!" – Dr. Sandra C. Duru

There's A Season Of Rest Ahead - Hold On To Your Faith!

Many times in life, we genuinely feel like throwing in the towel and giving up on everything we've strived for and pursued passionately. This is a normal human reaction, my dear, so you have nothing to worry about if it's upon you presently.

However, I need you to know that you are responsible for your mind and well-being to ensure you don't allow yourself to dwell too long in that state of mind. Remember that nothing lasts forever; hence, these bad patches you're going through are temporary hitches that will soon fade away.

There is a season of rest ahead, my love, but you must hold on to your faith and never stop believing that HE will keep you victorious through these dark times and seasons. You will enter your rest, my dear. HE has promised, and HE never fails!

Day 171

"You will never know your full potential unless you push yourself to find it. No man or woman is living who isn't capable of being more and doing more than is expected of him or her. All they need to do is put their mind to achieving greatness against all odds." – Dr. Sandra C. Duru

There Is Nothing You Cannot Achieve - Push Yourself And Be Amazed!

My beloved, how are you today? I am always quick to remember this scripture talking about the immense power and possibilities available to you as a person and the truth that absolutely nothing is impossible for you when you set your heart to it!

"And the LORD said, Behold, the people is one, and they have all one language; and this they begin to do: and now nothing will be restrained from them, which they have imagined to do." - Genesis11:6. Please observe one vital thing in this passage: This truth was revealed by the Lord God, the Maker and Creator of all things Himself! Now, my question is: If your car manufacturer says that your car model can travel at speeds exceeding 100 kph, do you doubt, argue, or disbelieve it?

Nature's voice to you today is pretty simple and direct, my love: There is absolutely nothing you cannot achieve in life, no matter what the circumstances, situations, and challenges standing against you may look like! All you need to do is dare to attempt and push yourself, and you will be amazed at the results you will effortlessly achieve!

Day 172

"Mistakes are part of your natural growing process, and you must never be afraid to make them because that is the only way to learn. Only ensure that you are learning from every mistake you make so that you do not repeat the same error many times." – Dr. Sandra C. Duru

That Mistake Can Prove To Be Fatal For You. Here's Why!

My love, some days ago, I shared nature's voice and inspiration with you regarding how mistakes are vital to your growth in so many ways and why you must embrace and never shy away from them instead of trying so hard to avoid them.

Today, however, I would like to create a balance by letting you know one fundamental truth, too. While making mistakes can be great for you, the entire purpose and reason why it's good for you becomes defeated if you do not learn from each one you make and improve.

This is why many people make the same mistakes repeatedly, which can be very dangerous for you, especially in specific fields of endeavor and practice. So, yes, that mistake can prove fatal if you refuse to learn from it and keep repeating it consistently!

May God deliver us from errors that would have no remedy, like Judas made by selling out on Jesus for 30 pieces of silver. When he sought to make amends, he was cast away and disgraced by the same people who lured him into it in the first place. Please don't go over the edge before recalling and saving yourself, my dear friend.

Day 173

"Don't try to understand why you are being misunderstood, attacked, or maltreated. Only bear in mind that the enemy is out to destroy you, and all you need to do is fight back intelligently, smartly, strategically, and get your escape route cleared up for the emergency exit." – Dr. Sandra C. Duru

Clear Up Your Escape Route Smartly - Stop Waiting For Explanations!

Have you ever studied how many animals react when you've chased them around for a long time and eventually have them cornered? Their instinct for survival and self-preservation will make them turn on their assailants and attempt to battle it out!

This primordial nature and instinct are in every one of God's creations, and I believe it's high time you start taping into and using yours as well. Stop being a victim always, even if you're consistently plagued and harassed on every side, and start thinking like a survivor and warrior!

There's no point asking the enemy why he wants to destroy you and see you fail always - that's his sole purpose in life! Instead of crying like a victim all the time, brace up, prepare, and smartly clear up an escape route for yourself, and, by all means, stop looking for or waiting for explanations from people who are obviously up to no good against you!

Your salvation and escape are the only things that matter. So get to it immediately, and may God help and be with you. Amen!

Day 174

"You can either become discouraged by failure or learn from it. So, go ahead and make mistakes. Make all you can because that is where you will find success." – Dr. Sandra C. Duru

Failure Can Produce Two Results In You - What Will It Be?

My love, an interesting and fun fact in life is that failures, setbacks, mistakes, and shortcomings have the tendency and power to produce one of two things in everyone - inspiration or depression.

The critical question now is, what would it bring out in you? Do you crawl into a shell of sadness when you fail to hit a target, or does it spur you to keep pushing until you get it done?

There's another fun fact I want you to know today, my dear: Every great person you know and celebrate today, living or departed, all failed and made terrible mistakes in their quest for success before achieving their purpose in life.

The difference is that they used their shortcomings as fuel to keep pursuing their goals, learned vital things from their mistakes and never repeated them, and refused to quit until they achieved their dreams. So, my dear, what will it be for you today?

Voice Of Nature (Vol.1) By Sandra Duru

Day 175

"Many times, bad and bitter people don't even need a genuine reason or an excuse to be mad at you and start wishing you evil. Keep your guard up always!" – Dr. Sandra C. Duru

An Evil Person Never Needs A Reason - Stay Guarded Always!

One very terrible thing about life that I have come to see too often and understand deeply, my love, is that an evil person needs no provocation, cause, or genuine reasons to attack and destroy you if you let them.

The spirit at work in them is of the enemy whose only mission and purpose is "to steal, to kill, and to destroy." Hence, you must always be on your guard around such people because their only happiness and joy are seeing others cry and anguish, even if you're the kindest and nicest person they've ever known.

Please, always remember, my love, that an evil person never needs a reason to attack you, so you must remain guarded always!

Day 176

"Do not follow someone else's path or live the life of others because they do not have the same destiny as you. You are very unique, and you have a unique destiny. Be real and honest with yourself." – Dr. Sandra C. Duru

Stop Following Others And Copying Them - You Are Unique!

Do you know that one of the best things that has ever happened to me was discovering my uniqueness and special nature at a tender age and sticking to it doggedly to this very day?

Oh, yes, it is, my dear. I do not mince words or hold back as I tell you again right now that following others about, copying them, and refusing to discover, harness, and develop your unique gifts and God-given abilities is a direct attack on yourself and the most foolish thing you can ever do in life!

Please, my dear friend, you are one of a kind, and there can never be another you, no matter how identical you are with anyone else! Do not rob the world of the uniqueness and special gifts the Creator has deposited inside you, my dear.

Always be authentic to yourself, and you will surely achieve immense greatness and success in life, no matter the obstacles or oppositions you face in your journey to your purpose.

Day 177

"You must live actively, take initiative, create discipline, make an effort, change, and grow beyond your imagination. Navigate these horrors, pains, and disappointments successfully to be your best." – Dr. Sandra C. Duru

The Best Of You Is Yet To Be Seen - Break Out Of The Cage Of Pain Today!

My love, are you aware that one of the primary reasons why you've been put through so much torment, pain, rejection, disappointments, and sadness is because of the greatness of your God-given purpose and destiny?

As hard as this may be to digest for many of you right now, you need to please understand that the only purpose the enemy attacks you is to break you and shatter your self-belief and will to live and succeed.

Hence, you must consciously decide to shame him by tapping into the limitless powers and resources the Creator has deposited in your mind, break out of the cage of pain all your terrible experiences have shackled you in all these years.

The best of you is yet to be seen; my love and creation await your glorious manifestation. Rise and break free today, my dear, and your shine will never know no limits or bounds!

Day 178

"Success is never for the faint-hearted or lazy people. It is for the tenacious, relentless, dogged, persistent, and never-say-die people who do not understand what the word 'impossible' means." – Dr. Sandra C. Duru

You Must Be Ignorant Of One Thing To Succeed In Life - Here It Is!

I'm sure you're wondering how ignorance can produce anything as vital and good as success in your life, my dear, but yes, it certainly can, and here is how.

Sadly, many people do not achieve much because they've become too knowledgeable for their Maker. Hence, when HE says that they are limitless and there's nothing they cannot achieve, they begin to rationalize, examine, and try to figure out how or why their Creator's word should be so.

My dear, success is only for those who do not know or refuse to understand what the word "impossible" means. There are countless evidences of many great people to back this up throughout humanity's history.

How will your story be written at the end of your time here on Earth, my dear? Will you be the one who knew too much and restricted their success, or the dogged "ignorant" ones who refused to understand limitations and impossibilities? The choice, again, is yours, my love..

Day 179

"As long as you have the spirit of discernment, you will never make the wrong decisions or choices. When you feel something isn't right or going well, please deal with it immediately and keep moving. No sentiments!" – Dr. Sandra C. Duru

You Have The Gift Of Discernment For A Reason - Never Ignore It!

My beloved, do you know that I cannot count how many times my family and I have been saved from impending disasters and even had terrible accidents averted before they happened because of this gift called discernment?

That "gut feeling" and intuition about specific people, places, and things did not just pop randomly into your head and mind. It is a function of that gift of discernment, and you must never ignore it!

You may sometimes feel like you're just imagining things or being paranoid, but I assure you that you are not today, my dear. Please begin to pay better attention to these feelings and nudges in your spirit, and you will be amazed at how many mistakes and sticky situations you will start to avoid and escape.

What do you even have to lose? After all, it is better to be safe than sorry, right??

Day 180

"When you learn new things, meet new people, change old beliefs, and discard useless thoughts, it exercises your thinking power to the extreme, and it will help you to grow." – Dr. Sandra C. Duru

New Things And Beliefs Are Good For You - Keep Reinventing Yourself!

Hello, my love. Are you aware that one of the essential qualities that visiting new places, making new friends, and gaining new knowledge consistently does to you is that it gives you good exposure, which in turn helps you to keep improving and bettering yourself?

This is called reinvention, my dear, and everything in nature must constantly evolve and reinvent itself lest it become obsolete and irrelevant in any field the Creator has placed it in.

You must continually examine, prune, and purge yourself of ideologies, mindsets, knowledge, and ways that do not befit or strengthen your God-given purpose in any way, my dear. Such reinventions are crucial to your success; hence, you must never be found wanting regarding them always.

Day 181

"Appreciate who you are and where you come from. Be proud of your culture and honor your uniqueness; pass it on to the next generation. Don't ever be ashamed of your roots and where you originate from. A river that forgets its source and tries to disconnect from it will dry up, remember?" - Dr. Sandra C. Duru

A Person Ashamed Of Their Heritage Lacks Wisdom - Don't Become Such!

I know that this is a fundamental truth the voice of nature has also mentioned earlier, but the truth is that it is a vital part of our existence that can never be overemphasized or spoken too much of!

A sad thing that obtains these days, especially among many of this younger generation, is an alarming reluctance and outright refusal to identify with their roots, tribes, cultural heritage, and backgrounds. This stems from an equally appalling trend and desires to copy other cultures and be what they're not created and designed to be; hence nature's constant admonitions!

Nothing disconnected from its source can ever continue to grow on its own. This is what becomes of you when you refuse to appreciate, embrace, and be proud of your heritage and natural uniqueness. Please know today that anyone who does and lives like this significantly lacks wisdom, and you must never be like such!

QUARTERLY SELF-APPRAISAL | REVIEW

(1) Mention at least two things you know you did better than last quarter.

(2) What would you regard as your biggest limitations or challenges so far, and how have you been facing them?

(3) Are you still behind on any of your set goals, dreams, and objectives this quarter?

(4) On a scale of 1-10, rate the level of success you've been able to achieve during the last quarter, and why you think you deserve your allotted mark.

(5) What would you consider to be your most significant achievement this last quarter?

QUARTER 3:

DAY 182 - DAY 273

Day 182

> *"Just because you went to school, got a degree, and got certified does not qualify you to teach. You must have the gift and compassion. The gift, the calling, the compassion, and the anointing will stand you out and make your job easier and stress-free, and you will feel fulfilled at the end of the day."* – Dr. Sandra C. Duru

You Need To Be Called To Teach - It Takes More Than Certification!

There was a time when this world focused more and rewarded competence and technical know-how over credentials and paper qualification, which was glorious!

You never had to worry about hiring or delegating things to someone because you were always confident about their efficiency based on visible competence. I would love things to return to that way, especially with the recruitment of teachers in our institutions of learning across all levels - creche to college.

There's a level of passion, a desire to birth and enlighten others, and a calling it takes to be placed over others as a teacher because it is such a vital role. If you don't have any of these qualities, please forget that piece of paper called your certificate that says you're qualified and look into another endeavor, my love.

You would only be doing it for the paycheck, and with teaching, you will undoubtedly have much more frustration than any joy in dealing with your students. You and your students deserve so much better in life, don't you agree?

Day 183

"Are you in the habit of giving more information on how things can be done, how you want to do it, and how you did it than the results? Learn to be results-oriented and let your success rate your efforts and sacrifices." - Dr. Sandra C. Duru

Let Your Success Speak - Your Work Is Loud Enough.

My love, I cannot help but remember a version of this famous adage from the South-Southern people of Nigeria, Africa, who say: "Your actions speak so loud, we can't hear what you are saying."

Learn and adopt this mentality in all you do, my dear, especially in your work and businesses. You don't need to spend all your time and energy explaining complex operations processes to anyone when your perfect deliveries and successes can take care of that for you.

Always focus on delivering the best results in anything you do, my dear, and the world will cease to query but consistently celebrate you instead.

Day 184

"No matter where you were born, or what you were born with, you are your only limitation, and it starts to show from how you handle seeming defeats, failures, mistakes and falls in life." – Dr. Sandra C. Duru

How You Handle Defeats Matter - Nobody Can Stop You But You!

My beloved, I want to believe that you already know by now that nothing on this Earth can stop, derail, or destroy your dreams, goals, and God-given purpose if you don't quit on yourself, right?

The circumstances, challenges, battles, and extremely tough situations surrounding you do not matter. They will never be able to break or ruin you unless you choose to wallow in them instead of rising above them!

No amount of shortcomings, mistakes, or defeats can ever stop a person from a dogged pursuit of their divine purpose in life because such things are normal and bound to happen. How you handle them, though, is what determines your eventual end.

Will it be one of great victory, testimonies, and celebrations, or otherwise? It's all up to you, my dear.

Day 185

"There's something very unique about you. Stop living a fake life, trying to be like someone else, trying to please people, or trying to follow the trend and miss the path to your expected destination." – Dr. Sandra C. Duru

A Copycat Will Never Find Their Destiny - Don't Waste Your Life!

There is something about nature and how it reaches out to us all, my dear, and I have become accustomed to it well enough over the years. Whenever it keeps returning to something, it may be because of just one or a few people who genuinely need constant admonitions to get out and break free from a terrible hold!

Please know and hear this again today, my love: Those who follow trends instead of discovering their unique purpose and pursuing it doggedly can never fulfill their destiny! Sadly, such lives can be counted as wasted because they would only exist through life instead of truly living and making the remarkable positive impacts they were created for.

My love, please don't be a copycat in life. You deserve and are created for much better things than being a mindless minion!

Day 186

"Man was not created for money, but money was created for the man. Hence, no man should ever be caught in this world's debasing worship of money." – Dr. Sandra C. Duru

Those Who Worship Money Have Lost Their Way - Don't Be Like Them!

Hello, my beloved. Do you know one interesting fact about money and why an obsessive craze for it is both senseless and detrimental? It is because money was created to serve you and not vice versa!

The moment you become so obsessed with amassing way more of it than you and yours could ever need per time, you are subtly sliding into the love and worship of money, and this is what even the scripture describes as "the root of all evil." And, isn't it right?

Guard your heart and guide your desires right, my dear. Having money is excellent and, indeed, not a bad thing. However, once you're desperate and can do anything to make a quid, you've gone over the edge and must retrace your steps immediately!

Day 187

"Learn to believe in yourself, your work, and your abilities. Above all, have faith in God Almighty and in your inner strength. Spark up your confidence and fuel your dreams with your tears. Yes, it's okay to cry when you fall hard, but don't ever wallow in self-pity and condemnation." – Dr. Sandra C. Duru

Those Tears Can Be Your Fuel - Belief In Yourself!

My beloved, have you ever been told that only the weak and helpless cry? This could not be farther from the truth, and you must rid yourself of such a debasing and limiting mindset today.

Yes, you must never allow yourself to become an object of pity and ridicule for your shortcomings. However, you must also know that taking some quiet moments to grieve over your losses and defeats can only make you better because those sober moments of reflection will help you see clearer and learn quickly from your mistakes.

Those tears can fuel you to your desired success as long as you never stop believing in yourself, my love. So, cry all you want to, but don't ever stop or think of quitting!

Day 188

"The dead no longer sulk or worry about any shortcomings, tribulations, rejections, or failures they face. Only the living can deal with such problems, and the fact that you're still alive means that you can still turn everything around and come out on top in the long run!"
– Dr. Sandra C. Duru

You Can Complain Because You're Still Alive - Be Grateful And Focused!

When was the last time you walked through a cemetery, attended a funeral, or visited a morgue, my love? Even the thought makes your belly turn right now, doesn't it?

However, do you know such excursions can do you way better than any jolly moments you could ever have? When you go to these places and see those who have departed, you're reminded of your great advantage over them - they are dead and gone, but you're still alive and can still achieve your dreams, goals, and purpose!

Regardless of your opposition and battles, always understand that being alive to fight is still the most incredible gift and a sign that you're not defeated or a failure. Hence, you must never quit on yourself and always focus on the positives around you because this is the only way to reach your destined greatness and purpose!

Day 189

"If you think positively and feel positive emotions, it shows on your face and interactions. People pick up on it, respond positively, and your life turns around." – Dr. Sandra C. Duru

A Positive Mind Begets A Positive Countenance - Stay Happy Always.

My love, if there's also one fallacy you must avoid with everything in you, it is that saying that you cannot be happy all the time because you can! Yes, you can, and I'll show you how.

Happiness, for humans, is mainly derived from the things we see, achieve, acquire, or receive. Hence, it is primarily tied to external factors, and that's where your power comes in. No matter what you get, see, or receive, you can maintain a cheerful heart by always being thankful for all you've enjoyed in life, and this contagious mindset will spin over into everything about you.

So, my dear, always remember that a positive mind begets a positive attitude, and others around you always sense your vibes, which determines how they interact with you. That cheerful spirit may be all you need to gain the favor and help for your next level and phase in life. Stay happy always, my dear!

Day 190

"You are not too small, poor, or young to start being an influencer wherever you find yourself. You can commit yourself to being one of the people to champion a good cause in your community by reaching out to the sick, hungry, and so many other people in need in your little way." – Dr. Sandra C. Duru

There Are No Small Influencers, Only Small Minds.

Have you ever been told that you don't need money, fame, great wealth, or anything to impact your environment and immediate community positively? No, you don't, my dear.

Some of the most influential people to have ever lived didn't have a penny to their name and were not even famous or known before they began the type of impact the world noticed them for.

Today, the world remembers and celebrates people like Mahatma Gandhi, Mother Theresa, Mary Slessor, and others for dedicating their lives to the cause of bettering that of others. What will you be remembered for when you are no more, my love?

Day 191

"This is no time to drown yourself in tears; neither is it the time to wallow in self-pity or regrets. Rather, it's the time to heal. And for you to heal, you must first forgive yourself, and then forgive the one that hurt you."
– Dr. Sandra C. Duru

Forgive Yourself And Move On - That's The Only Way To Heal!

When terrible things happen to us, it's normal to withdraw into a reclusive shell and drown ourselves in our sorrow and tears. Yes, I admit that it is, and you're not in error or weak if you've ever done or are still doing this presently.

As nature's voice said a few days ago, it is good to mourn your losses and have moments of sober reflection. However, please do not linger in such reflective and mourning shells, as they have the potential and power to do you more significant harm than any good!

The only way to heal from the pain, betrayal, bitterness, anger, and anguish is to forgive yourself and those who hurt you and move on. Remember, you need it more for you than for them, and you must always be your number one priority, my love?

Day 192

"You may think you're trying to save someone from troubles and heartaches by telling lies, pretending, or sweet-talking them, only to find out you only succeeded in compounding their problems. Don't be the reason for another person's woes. Say the truth always." – Dr. Sandra C.Duru

Lies And Flattery Never Help - Don't Indulge Them!

My love, have you ever been in a situation where you tried to make things better but ended up making it far worse than before because of the line of action or even the choice of words you used?

This is not only possible, but it's the exact thing that happens whenever you decide to tell a lie, deceive, or flatter anyone because you think it would bell them not to know the truth. That is so wrong, my love. It is only the truth that has the power to make anything free.

So, no matter what happens, decide to and only speak the truth always, no matter whose ox gored, and you will save the situation way better than you could ever imagine!

Day 193

"Don't ever let the things that you don't have today weigh you down, get you depressed, and prevent you from seeing the ones you have, no matter how little or seemingly insignificant they are!" – Dr. Sandra C. Duru

Always Focus On The Right Things - You Have More Than You Know!

The one thing many people do these days that gets them into depression and hopelessness faster is to keep allowing the enemy to shift their attention and focus on the wrong things around them.

Don't ever fall for this age-old, cheap trick, my love! No matter how insignificant those so-called "little wins" are, remember that many people worldwide may not have achieved them yet and may never do.

Hence, you should remain proud and happy about them and keep your eyes on those things that matter - the positives, instead of allowing your mind to wander to and dwell on negativities most times.

Day 194

"You need to forgive the one who hurt you; it is the sweetest revenge! When people maltreat you, and you pay back with forgiveness, it kills them!" – Dr. Sandra C. Duru

Forgiveness Is The Best Revenge - Try It Today!

My beloved, have you ever been privileged to look into the eyes of someone who had tormented and terribly maltreated you and see how they react when you treat them with kindness and compassion instead of the judgment they deserve?

I have done this countless times, and I assure you that there's almost no satisfaction more remarkable than seeing the shame in their eyes when the realization hits them that you're not going after your point of flesh.

The best revenge you can ever exert on anyone is forgiveness, my darling, and I would love for you to begin to try it today! And, also remember these excellent words in the scriptures: "Therefore if thine enemy hunger, feed him; if he thirst, give him drink: for in so doing thou shalt heap coals of fire on his head. Be not overcome of evil, but overcome evil with good." - Romans 12:20-21.

Now, pray tell, what better way to get back at anyone could you ever come up with that trumps this?

Day 195

"God has a peculiar way of keeping HIS own, my dear, and this so-called delay you're experiencing may just be HIS little way of hiding you in a safe corner until you're ripe enough for the glory you seek." – Dr. Sandra

Stay Hidden Until You're Ripe - It's For Your Good!

Are you aware that the reason why many birds continue to brood and watch over their infants till they're well grown is not only to help them stand on their feet but also to protect and keep them alive for as long as possible?

Any chick that refuses to stay under the mother's protection and continually wanders off on its own will swiftly become a meal for the next available predators it happens to meet prematurely!

This applies to you, too, my love, and I urge you to please remain calm and pay attention, even as you continue to abide in that hiding place God has kept you. It's for your good, my dear, and not because HE doesn't want to answer your prayers or grant your requests.

Please stay hidden until you are ripe for the attention, pressure, and scrutiny your God-given purpose will surely bring when you succeed at it. I repeat - it is for your good!

Day 196

"Never leave till tomorrow what can be done today because no one is assured of tomorrow. Life is so fickle, so you must cherish your life before it's taken away from you." – Dr. Sandra C. Duru

Do All You Can Today - Tomorrow Is Never Guaranteed!

One of the most significant harms many of us do to ourselves is to believe that we still have a lot of time on Earth, so we don't take our missions and purposes as seriously and urgently as we should.

This trick that "you still have a lot of time and will always catch up" is a satanic lie that has lured and eventually destroyed many, and I hope as you read this today, you will escape from such manipulations of the enemy.

Everything about your life on Earth is unpredictable, and no one knows their appointed departure dates but only know we will all surely go one day. Don't waste today and this moment procrastinating and pushing for later what can be done now.

Do all you can today, my love, because tomorrow is certainly not assured!

Day 197

"Don't judge your achievement based on anyone else's standard because you are not wired the same way. Everyone has their destiny and peculiarity." – Dr. Sandra C. Duru

You Are The Only Standard - Stop Looking At Others!

My beloved, do you know that one of the fastest and surest ways to belittle and shortchange yourself in life is to make the life of others the parameters, gauge, and standards by which you judge your life?

Your divine uniqueness forbids such folly, my dear, and you should know this well by now, please. Never weigh or check your success against what anyone else has done before you. You are the only standard your life has; hence, you must stop looking at others, no matter who they are or what they have achieved.

As your gifts and purpose are uniquely assigned to you, so will your judgment before your Creator when you transit this realm. So, living by anyone else's standards or doctrine besides HIS is a great folly and a certain undoing for you, my dear.

Day 198

"The way up in life is, first of all, downward before you can shoot up. Before sprouting and growing tall, trees grow deep into the ground first, remember?" – Dr. Sandra C. Duru

Nothing Grows Without Going Down First - Don't Panic!

My love, how familiar are you with nature and how things work when you plant any seed? Have you ever wondered where that seed grows first, or you've always believed they only grow upwards when planted?

Well, my dear, there's a reason why the initial process is called "taking roots" in the soil - that seed must establish a base in the ground first before it can sprout. Even more interesting, though, is that every seed must die first after you bury them in the soil before they can reproduce the desired harvest. Isn't nature and our Creator fantastic?

Stop fretting about what seems like a period or phase of "deadness" or lack of visible growth in your life, my love. Your sprouting is assured if you put in the proper work and effort to continue developing yourself. In due time, you, too, shall yield a bountiful harvest of results, victories, testimonies, and remarkable accomplishments!

Nothing grows up without going down first, so don't panic, my dear friend.

Day 199

"No matter how tough or challenging the obstacles before you may be, always remember that it is more dangerous for you to delay your needed moves than it is to face them head-on." – Dr. Sandra C. Duru

Procrastination Is Deadlier Than Those Perceived Battles - Take Them On!

I remember a story in the Scriptures about some lepers outside Samaria's gates during the terrible famine because of a mighty siege laid against the city in the days of Elisha the prophet.

The nation's deliverance came through those lepers because they dared to advance against the seemingly terrible enemy they could see instead of waiting and doing nothing. In their words (paraphrased), "If they wait at the city's gates, they will die of hunger. If they went into the enemy's camp, they would get slain. However, they may get food before dying in the enemy's camp, so why wait in fear and still die of hunger at the gates?"

As you read the book of 2 Kings 7 for context, please remember the important lesson here, my love: Procrastination is a worse and deadlier enemy than all those obstacles and battles seemingly stacked against you. Hence, you must never slack or be afraid to make your move and take them all on!

Your Creator expects a level of faith and actions from you before HE moves everything in nature in your favor many times. Don't be caught slagging, my dear! Your appointed time for victory is now.

Day 200

"Don't ever show any weakness, and never give anyone the pleasure of lording anything over your life. Prove to them that you are your ship's captain and have hopes and aspirations that must and will be fulfilled."
– Dr. Sandra C. Duru

Your Life Is Your Ship, And You Are The Captain - Never Forget That!

Many conditions, situations, and circumstances may befall a person, making them become a shadow of themselves and timid in life. Yes, I know this very well because I have been through and conquered this, too, my love.

One thing that helped me immensely, and I want to share with you today, is that you must always keep your head high, no matter what! You are the captain of this ship called your life, and as long as you're alive and at the helm, none of your dreams, visions, and goals will ever become a failure!

This is the mindset I doggedly held on to and kept pressing on, and today, my life inspires millions worldwide. Yours can and will be the same if you'll always stand firm and never allow anyone to turn you into an object of pity and ridicule.

Day 201

"Your scar symbolizes power and resilience – Do not let the enemy turn it into an object of depression and sadness for you. It shows just how far you've come and the pain you've had to go through and conquer to get here today." – Dr. Sandra C. Duru

Scars Are Not Shameful - Stop Hiding Yours.

My beloved, there are a few things in life that you should never be ashamed of if you have them, and, for me, scars remain one of the top things on that list.

A battle-tested and proven warrior can never come without scratches, cuts, and scars. That is the evidence that you've been through the fire, come through the flood, and you're still standing tall and strong.

Scars are not shameful things or objects of ridicule, my love; hence, you must never hide yours from anyone again! Wear them with pride, and keep your head up as you achieve your dreams and fulfill your purpose.

You are not only a survivor but a conqueror, too. So, what's there not to be bold about and proud of?

Day 202

"Forgiveness is always for you and not for the object of your pain, suffering, or anger. When you forgive, a burden is lifted off your chest, and you can move on with your life without needless baggage." – Dr. Sandra C. Duru

Forgive And Be Free - Rid Yourself Of Needless Baggage!

Do you know that for every hurt, pain, an offense against you, and slight that you refuse to forgive and end up becoming bitter about, you have just granted the enemy more than enough room to live in your head rent-free and continue wreaking havoc?

There is a burden that unforgiveness, bitterness, hatred, and anger pile upon our spirits whenever we hold on to them and refuse to let go. They are corrosive elements that will always cause more harm and no good at all!

Please rid yourself of such needless baggage, my love, and enjoy a free, healthy, and mentally stable life by letting go of all hurt against you in forgiveness today. It is for your good, my dear.

Day 203

"Do you know that for every hurt, pain, an offense against you, and slight that you refuse to forgive and end up becoming bitter about, you have just granted the enemy more than enough room to live in

Your Greatness Requires Only One Thing - Here It Is!

Hello, my love. Are you aware that the key to your success and greatness in life is not tied to any resources or connections you can ever have but, first of all, knowing your God-given purpose on earth?

Having this knowledge and then fully committing yourself to pursue and fulfill it is the most significant decision you can ever make. And I assure you that if you do this today, you are already halfway there and must surely achieve your dreams and goals!

This is the most vital thing your greatness requires, my dear. A life without purpose is one wasted already because once the purpose is not known, abuse is certainly inevitable! Find yours today, and your future and greatness are guaranteed and secured.

Day 204

"Wait for your time so you don't jump the gun and get disqualified from the race. Wait for your time; the whistle will blow, and you'll run your race. God's time is the best!" – Dr. Sandra C. Duru

There Is A Set Time For Everything - Wait For Yours!

My dear friend, one thing that has always fascinated me about nature is the way daytime and night never cease to flow in and out of each other seamlessly.

What's even more interesting is that none of us have ever woken up one day and started worrying about how the sun would set that day or how the next day would break, or have you?

I'm confident you have never had to do that, so the question is, why are you so worried about your time of rest, success, and breakthrough in life, too? The Creator has promised, my dear, and HE never fails!

There is a set time for everything, my beloved. Wait for yours, and I assure you that it will undoubtedly come, and you will be celebrated and glorified as you achieve your life goals.

Day 205

"The darkest hours of the night are the few ones before the break of dawn. Hence, do you know that the phase of your life when it seems like the battle is going to crush you if you don't quit and bow before it is the very moment when your glory is about to be revealed?" – Dr. Sandra C.Duru

The Fight Is Always Hardest Toward The End - Don't Relent!

My love, one of the most disturbing images I've ever seen remains one of two men digging through a treasure-filled cave, hoping to find some.

The illustration shows one man quitting and walking away sad when he was just one more throw off his digger to strike a pile of diamonds, while the other man took one more swing and hit the jackpot.

No matter how hard and unbearable it may seem, please never think of relenting in this battle called life because you never can tell what the next blow you land can break through for you!

Remember that the fight is always most challenging when it's about to end, so you must keep pushing through and never quit. History only records and remembers victors, not quitters. Hence, you must never relent, and you shall also be celebrated sooner than later, my dear.

Day 206

"Life is not a bed of roses. It is full of ups and downs. So, whenever you are faced with your downtimes, learn not to allow it to affect you. Learn from the challenges because that's where you'll draw your success story from." – Dr. Sandra C. Duru

Your Strength Comes From Those Challenges - Don't Let Them Break You!

Have you ever been told that you can never become the champion your Creator had destined you to be without passing through these fiery trials, tribulations, and tests you're dealing with presently?

Yes, my love. You can never be a champion without facing and overcoming different battles, and these tests are to bring forth your testimonies, not to destroy you! So, please, my dear, I need you to understand and know this surely from today.

These tests, challenges, and trials are where your strength comes from. Hence, you must embrace and never let them break you! They are sure things you must encounter and overcome in life, but as you do, you become better and are promoted.

So, why run from your guaranteed promotions and blessings, my dear? Embrace them!

Day 207

"Many times, the reason you tend to struggle with achieving your goals and daily tasks is that you put things till later, thinking you have all the time in the world. No, you do not!" – Dr. Sandra C. Duru

You Don't Have The Luxury Of Time – Do It Now!

My beloved, how are you today? If there is another thing that nature's voice cannot over-emphasize to us daily, it is the truth that none of us have the luxury of time in this life!

No, you don't, my dear. So, you see that great dream that your mind keeps telling you that you may not have the suitable capacity to pursue yet? Do it now! That vision that looks like you may never be able to begin because you "need time" to gather resources for it - do it now!

Don't let the enemy rob you by deceiving you that you still have time to pursue these things later. Do them now, my dear, because you don't have such luxuries; hence, you cannot afford to waste any more precious seconds. Start now!

Day 208

"Take time out to study yourself – your passions, cravings, desires, and those things that you seem to be able to do quite easily and enjoy doing a lot. The answer to your calling may be hidden in those seemingly little things." – Dr. Sandra C. Duru

Your Purpose Is Hidden In Your Desires - Explore Them!

My love, one of the most significant errors we make in life is chasing the wrong dreams, visions, and goals and leaving our God-given purpose and talents behind because we're trying to make ends meet.

For many people, though, they do this because they don't even know what their purpose and true calling in life is. However, the voice of nature resides in all of us, and it softly calls to our hearts daily. You can never miss your way if you are calm enough to listen to it!

What is that thing, or are those few things that you seem to be able to do quite well, even without any real formal training, and can never picture yourself living without doing? They say that such things are your passion, but the voice of nature says this is your true calling, and your purpose is tied to those things.

Your purpose in life is hidden in your desires, so you must take your time to study yourself and explore them, and you will begin to prosper as you develop and start utilizing them.

Day 209

"When life takes you on a bumpy ride, and everything around you seems to be going wrong, don't give up. Keep your hopes high, because that point where your anxiety level rises, and you are contemplating giving up, is the very point of your turn around." – Dr. Sandra C. Duru

Don't Give Up Because The Road Is Rough - What Will Your Testimony Be?

There is a famous saying I love so much - "When the going gets tough, the tough get going." Oh, I have been on this path too many times already, my dear, and I know it's not an easy road!

However, do you know that it is only through this path that you can get to your glorious destiny; hence, you must never run away from it?

When the road gets rough and tough, you must never quit or give up, my dear. What will your testimony be at the end of your time here if all you do is quit and give up in the face of trouble? Think about this today, my love, and may God strengthen you...Amen!

Day 210

"No one is assured or guaranteed any extra second in life, no matter how much we wish and all pray to grow old and grey. Live in this realization every day of your life, and you will be amazed at the number of things you will get done easily." – Dr. Sandra C. Duru

You Will Achieve More When You Realize One Thing - Know This Truth!

My beloved, have you ever been opportuned to spend time with people or anyone with a terminal disease or been to a cell block to visit anyone on death row?

I tell you, such experiences are crucial to your growth and mental toughness! Why? Well, one thing these people have in common is that they know they are already on " borrowed time, " so they rarely waste a single second on meaningless things again.

Every second you spend in life is supposed to count for something good, productive, and helpful for your God-given purpose and vision here on Earth. What are your plans for today, and what have you done so far?

When you know this truth and walk in it daily, you will be amazed at how much you will begin to achieve effortlessly! What are you waiting for? Go on and give it a try today, my dear!!

Day 211

"It is not just enough to fight; the true joy is winning and learning. Don't give up before your miracle shows up. You have come this far already, so keep holding on and endure this to the end." – Dr. Sandra C. Duru

You Didn't Come This Far To Lose - You Can't Win If You Quit, Though!

Hello, my love. If there's one sure thing I have come to learn and profoundly know about life, it is that everything good you will ever achieve in it has to be obtained through diligence, persistence, hard work, and a good-old scrappy fight for each one of them.

You must be willing to fight for all your desires and see that battle to the end, too. It's not about how you start something, but what you learn from and how you finish it also matters greatly!

My dear, please know that you haven't come this far in life to lose. However, you cannot win if you quit or give up either. So, you must keep pushing and throwing those punches to the end, or it will have all been in vain. You wouldn't want that for yourself, now, would you?

Day 212

" Can you survive the rejection test? Can you keep fighting and moving on even after you've been publicly humiliated and disgraced? Sometimes, God allows this to happen for a reason and a season. Be encouraged!" – Dr. Sandra C. Duru

What Do You Do After Being Rejected Publicly?

My love, there are a few things in life that are very hard to swallow, and undoubtedly, public rejection, humiliation, and embarrassment are topmost on this list. However, what do you do after being humiliated and rejected like this?

Do you bow your head in shame, cave in, and walk away dejected? Or do you pick yourself up, dust yourself off, and take another crack at that dream, vision, or object of your desire again and again till you eventually break through?

Many times, these rejections and humiliations are allowed by God to see how we would react and also to test how much pride we still harbor inside us. Pride is an abomination to HIM, so you must lose all of you to have HIS fullness, as this is the only assurance of the victory and glory you seek in life.

So, I ask again, my dear, what will your reaction be?

Day 213

"You are different, and it's not your fault. You have a unique destiny, and you must embrace it. HE prepared you for this even before you were formed in your mother's womb." – Dr. Sandra C. Duru

Don't Be Sad Or Dejected For Being Different - Love Your Uniqueness!

In my journey through life, I have seen, encountered, and met many types of individuals, and the one thing I cherish in each of them is their unique gifts, characters, and qualities.

Ideally, these things set you apart and help you make the needed lasting impression on the people that matter to your life and destiny. I've also met many who still deal with me today because they saw something extraordinarily unique in me, and these qualities paved the path to success with them for me.

So, my love, nature seeks you to know and understand today that you must never be sad or discouraged because of your uniqueness. Instead, you must love and embrace it because, in all honesty, there is not and can never be another you!

Hence, my dear, you must celebrate and rejoice in your unique qualities and abilities.

Day 214

"If you don't appreciate and love yourself for who you are, how do you expect others to accept you? See, don't ever try to live by the dictates of others. It will only lead you to a life of regrets." – Dr. Sandra C. Duru

If You Don't Love Yourself, Others Will Hardly Ever Do!

One of the fastest ways to become depressed, dejected, and downcast in life is to try to please everyone around you to your detriment. This level of folly is as astounding as it is pathetic!

See, my love, if you do not love yourself, others around you will hardly ever do! Even sadder is that they will notice how less you value yourself, and many will exploit it to your pain, discomfort, and perpetual sadness.

You deserve way better than this in life, my dear. However, you must stand up for yourself and take what's rightfully yours already, and it all starts by placing a premium on yourself and living accordingly always!

Day 215

"How your life will turn out is entirely in your hands. You don't need anyone's approval to be whoever you want. So, dust yourself off, look in the mirror, and tell yourself, 'I'm Enough, I'm capable, I'm confident, and I won't let anyone make me feel little about myself!" – Dr. Sandra C. Duru

You Are Capable And More Than Enough - Do You Believe It?

Hello, my love. Have you ever taken time to sit and reflect on this profound truth of nature that says no force, power, or person on Earth can decide how and what you will turn out in life?

You are so capable and enough to achieve and become anything you set your mind on in life, my dear. Hence, you must never allow naysayers and those who seek to see you fail and destroyed the pleasure of seeing you fall or weak!

You are the captain of your life's ship and have more than it takes to navigate your way to immense glory and success. Do you believe this, my dear?

Day 216

"Do you know that people only relate with you the way you carry and present yourself? If you present yourself as strong, they relate with you as a strong person, and if you present yourself otherwise, that's exactly what you get." – Dr. Sandra C. Duru

There Are No Hidden Tricks To Life - What You See Is What You Get!

My love, are you aware that you may be the main reason why many people around you still look down on you and never take you seriously? Yes, you may be, and I will tell you how today.

See, my dear, people will readily buy a bottle of water at a cheaper rate from a roadside vendor but buy the same water at a more exorbitant rate in a lounge, club, or high-level hotel. They pay more for the same water because the other locations chose to properly brand themselves and their wares, while the roadside vendor remains unappreciated and cheap.

There are no hidden tricks in life, my dear; what you see is what you get! If all you think about and call yourself is a lizard or worm, don't expect anyone to see or call you a dinosaur! This is a simple law of nature; you must know and utilize it sufficiently to prosper and benefit from it.

Day 217

"Many of the challenges you face in life are either to avert a bigger evil or to pave the way for the blessings ahead. Life is full of ups and downs, and you must learn to enjoy the up times and endure the downtimes." – Dr. Sandra C. Duru

There Are Countless Seasons In Life - Learn To Enjoy Each One!

My beloved, the great Apostle Paul said something in his letter to the Phillipian Church that I love so much, and I want to share a profound truth from it with you today.

He said that, in all things, he knows how to live humbly and how to abound, too. This means he understands that there are countless seasons in life and has mastered the art of enjoying and living through each.

You must learn to do the same today and walk in this wisdom. No matter how hard you try, there will always be challenges and trials along your path in life. However, you must never forget that nothing lasts forever; hence, you should know how to take things in your stride and enjoy each season.

This is quite essential in so many ways, my love!

Day 218

"Don't worry if many people do not understand you. You are different, unique, and special. So, keep doing what you're doing, and God will always bless you because you are fulfilling your purpose, and that is all that matters." – Dr. Sandra C. Duru

Everyone Doesn't Have To Understand You - You're Not Wired For That!

Do you know that there is no way on this earth that everyone you meet will ever genuinely love, care for, and appreciate you, no matter what you do or how great you are at them?

See, my love, nature's truth to you today is pretty short but direct, and it has a lot of wisdom and power hidden in it: Everyone doesn't have to understand, appreciate, or love you in life! You are not even wired that way because of how unique the Creator made you, so stop seeking such from anyone!

The only thing that matters is HIM, and as long as you're living the life HE made you for, keep flowing, my darling. You are doing great and will be just fine at the end!

.

Day 219

"Look around you; there is always something to be grateful for. Count your blessings; see how they will always outweigh your troubles."
– Dr. Sandra C. Duru

Only Ingrates Never Maintain A Thankful Heart - There's Always Something!

My darling, do you know that, as long as you're alive and still breathing well today, there is already something extraordinary you should be thankful for?

Many struggle with gratitude and a consistent heart of thankfulness because of deep-seated ingratitude over what we feel we haven't received from our Maker.

Nothing can be more foolish than living this way, and you must never be caught in such a life and mindset, my dear! There is always something to be thankful for and genuinely grateful for. Please keep your eyes on those positives; you'll be amazed at how every negativity will fade away.

Day 220

"Your actions and agreements or confessions must align entirely for you to begin to ascend and dominate in life. In other words, you must walk it as you talk it, else, you may remain in the same spot for too long." – Dr. Sandra C. Duru

How Can Your Life Align With Your Declarations? This Is The Simplest Way!

Hello, my beloved. Are you aware that faith without works is dead; hence, everything you say and claim to believe must also reflect in your actions and the things you do consistently?

Yes, they must, my dear. Otherwise, all you will have are empty words of declarations that you continually make thanks and void with your inaction and lack of activity!

The Creator promised that HE would bless the works of your hands, but what happens when you have nothing to do for HIM to bless? You can't just talk about success always without walking and working towards it, my dear.

So, how can your life align with your declarations? Match your words with actions and walk the talk always, and you will surely live a life filled with testimonies and countless victories!

Day 221

"Always remember that we are all created differently, with something special in everyone. Discover yours and guard it jealously." – Dr. Sandra C. Duru

Your Path And Story Is Different - Don't Conform To What You're Not.

My love, how're you doing today? Do you know the most fascinating part of the history of Israel that I love? It is the stark contrast in everything between two of their greatest and most successful kings, who were father and son, too.

King David was a valiant man of war who, according to history, went to war over 1,000 times and never lost once! However, his son, King Solomon, never wielded a sword or shield but conquered and subdued his enemies through unparalleled wisdom, knowledge, and understanding.

Do you know that if Solomon had forcefully tried to follow in his father's footsteps, he would have died a premature, sad, and excruciating death in battle? Know your strengths, personality, and purpose, my dear, and please stick to it!

Your path and story are different, so you must never conform to what you are not. Don't die before your time, my darling.

Day 222

"Life throws many battles and challenges at us, but what you make of them and how you handle them will determine what you become. Will you be known as another one of life's victims, or would you be celebrated as a victor?" – Dr. Sandra C. Duru

You Can Either Be A Victor Or A Victim - You Decide!

My beloved, this is one fundamental truth that nature and everything in creation can never tell us enough. How do you handle afflictions, setbacks, tribulations, and trials?

Do you know that you can take life's brutal hits on the chin and keep bouncing back constantly, or you could quake and bend over in fear and never attempt anything meaningful again because "life was mean" to you? The choice is yours, my dear friend.

You can either be a victor or a victim in life, and the choice is no one else's but yours. Please choose wisely!

Day 223

"If there is one awesome thing you could ever do for yourself that would make you glad all the days of your life, it is to be yourself at all times and never to try to imitate anyone. Do you even realize that you are so special, and no one else on this planet could ever be you?" – Dr. Sandra

There Is Limitless Joy In Originality - Flaunt It!

A fantastic feature of nature that science has long revealed is that there are no two identical fingerprints, even if they belong to identical twins!

So, my question for you today, my dear, is it not insanity for you to now be trying to imitate someone the Creator deliberately ensured you have no similarities with? Why would you ever want to be an imitation or copy of anyone else when you were created and endowed with limitless unique qualities and abilities?

There is tremendous and limitless joy in originality, so you must always be proud and flaunt yours everywhere you find yourself! After all, there can never be another you, so why cower and be timid when you were destined to be so much more?

Day 224

"Yes, the power of death and life are in the tongue, but if you keep 'speaking things into existence' without taking any action, nothing tangible will ever come of it!" – Dr. Sandra C. Duru

Show Me Your Faith By Your Works, Not Words!

A few days ago, the voice of nature spoke to us about the significance of having something doing so that our Creator may have a tangible channel in our lives to bless us through.

I want to add this little scripture again today to re-emphasize this natural principle and show you how imperative it is! The Apostle James also concurs that faith without works is dead, but he takes it a step further.

He teaches us to "show faith by your works and not your words," because of what essence would it be to say that you believe strongly in something continually, yet you don't ever take any steps on it to prove you do?

Show your faith through your deeds, actions, and works, or your life will be filled with many declared but never manifested blessings!

Day 225

"The process may be very heartbreaking, rough, painful, and tough, but remember that life is the survival of the fittest, and you can allow yourself to either be molded or ruined by it." – Dr. Sandra C. Duru

Yes, The Process Is Rough, But Nobody Ever Said It Would Be Easy!

One of the worst things that can happen to any human on this Earth is to suffer the delusion and gross misconception that anything in this life comes easy. No, it is not, and it will never be.

However, this is not a statement to make you fear, lose confidence, and quit the fight because it's tough. You must keep fighting and never think of throwing in the towel because the Creator chose your path for a purpose!

Yes, it is very cumbersome, tiring, and filled with countless battles, but nobody ever said that life would be easy before, so why quake or get discouraged in the thick of things now, my love? Keep fighting!

Day 226

"The world needs your uniqueness. In your true identity and uniqueness lies your strength and the key to unlocking your success. Live your own life and not another person's life. Be you, and be proud of yourself. You can't operate like everyone else!" – Dr. Sandra C. Duru

Operating Like Someone Else Is A Huge Loss - To You And Humanity!

My love, have you ever thought about how this world would be right now if every gifted inventor God had created all saw the first inventor on earth and decided to be like him instead of following their unique paths?

For instance, if Graham Bell had been the first inventor with his invention of the telephone, how would we all be living today if other geniuses after him did not maintain their uniqueness and continued on their destined paths?

Come on, my dear. Trying to operate like someone else and be what you're not is a massive loss to yourself and the world! Be proud of your uniqueness and own it without flinching!

There's a place for all of us in nature, and we must do our bit to ensure we fulfill this God-given purpose to the letter.

Day 227

"Don't allow your mind, the engine house of your life, to be messed up. Once you have your mind under control, you can take care of the situation and come out of it better, stronger, and more successful." – Dr.Sandra C. Duru

Your Mind Is Invaluable In More Ways Than One - Protect It!

Do you know that there is nothing like an insurmountable mountain before you if your mind is right and you're not panicking whenever trouble hits?

Your mind is invaluable in more ways than one, my love; hence, I can never stop talking about it or encouraging you to protect it at all costs! Everything you are today and hope to achieve is rooted in and hugely dependent on the state of your mind and the quality of your consistent thoughts.

Nothing must mess with your mental health, and you must continually grow your mental toughness by pushing yourself to achieve anything hitherto impossible! You have no limits, my dear, so why not? After all, nothing is impossible for you.

Day 228

"Always remember that your actions carry much more weight than your words. They speak much louder than anything you may say with your words; hence, they must always align, and you must be consistent with this to see results." – Dr. Sandra C. Duru

Words Are Powerful, But So Are Your Actions!

What do you think would become of a person who says he will have a great life filled with wealth, good health, love, peace, and everything good in life yet refuses to get up from his bed every day?

Of course, your guess is as good as mine - he will end up with a life that matches his actions, not just his words! Whatever you do, my dear, please don't be like a confused person whose words and actions are like two opposite poles that never meet!

Not only must you say the things you want to see, but you must also ensure that your actions tally with them so that your flourishing may break forth like the sun, and then your profiting shall appear for all.

Day 229

"Once you get played into the corner of self-pity or hopelessness, your mind is completely messed up, caged, and will be ready for easy access to all sorts of manipulations, lies, negative influences, thoughts, and desperation kicks in. Never allow yourself to fall into this trap!" – Dr. Sandra C. Duru

Hopelessness Is Not For Champions And Kings - Avoid It!

My love, have you ever seen anyone who acts hastily without giving their words or actions any thought? Without a doubt, it would be challenging for such to break even, let alone accomplish any meaningful success in life!

Many times, though, acting rashly and impulsively can be traced to a mind filled with fear, hopelessness, and wallowing in self-pity! Please don't ever fall into the trap of being deceived by anyone about your journey through life and the unique path God had placed you on from creation.

Give no ear to negativity, toxic people, and naysayers around you, and never allow anyone to poison your mind about your capabilities and everything you already have. That you don't see the glory yet doesn't mean it's not there in you.

Never let anything poison your mind and spirit, my dear. Hopelessness is not synonymous with kings and champions; hence, you must avoid it diligently!

Day 230

"When you are born to inspire, motivate, impact, empower, lead, and transform, you will definitely be a very peculiar person. You have a unique destiny, and there's nothing anyone or any system can do about it." – Dr. Sandra C. Duru

The Destiny Determines The Character - Nothing Can Change You!

Are you aware that no matter how hard a lion tries, it can never live underwater or be crowned king of the seas and oceans, too, like in the jungle?

If, by its divine nature and programming, nothing can make that lion do against this ordinance of its Creator, no matter what, why are you allowing yourself to believe the lies of the enemy that you can amount to no good in life?

Your destiny determines your character, qualities, abilities, and personality; no power or alignment of any forces or even science can change or alter this!

So, rest assured, my dear, because your destiny will undoubtedly be fulfilled in due time, and that unique purpose will be achieved as long as you stay in this truth and believe nothing else but your Maker's voice through nature to you always.

Day 231

"Desperation can lead to anxiety and depression. Yes, it can cause you mental distress, agony, and disheartenment if you don't tie the knot and hold on whenever you find yourself at the rope's end. Don't give in to it!" – Dr. Sandra C. Duru

Never Give In To Desperation - Fight It!

My love, do you know that one of the significant causes of depression in many people today, especially young adults, is an inexplicable desperation to be successful and start achieving things early?

Many times, some of these people don't even have anything it takes to sustain the success they hungrily hunt and crave, yet they work themselves into terrible fits over it. Hence, you must remain grounded and never rush for anything, my dear.

The Creator says HE makes all things beautiful in HIS own time, not yours. So, you must always be wary lest you fall into desperation-induced anxiety over things you have no control over.

Never give room for desperation to grow in your spirit. Keep fighting it daily, and sooner than later, your appointed time will come, too, and your glory will be celebrated!

Day 232

"For you to actualize your vision and see your dreams come to reality, your actions must become one with your word. If all you do is talk about it and say it only but never take any action to back it up and progress it, it will never happen." – Dr. Sandra C. Duru

Nothing Happens With Words Only - Life Requires Action!

If four grown men were to sit around a table and talk about lifting that table and placing it at the other end of the room all day, where do you reckon the table will be when they all leave later that night?

Your guess ought to be as good as mine on this one - it will be on the same spot they all sat around it all day, my love! As funny as this may sound, this is what many of us do with our dreams, plans, visions, and projects almost all our lives.

All many people do is talk and talk, yet they keep wondering why nothing seems to be happening to them. Life requires action, my dear because nothing ever happens with words only! Translate those thoughts and words into action today, and you'll be happy to consistently see your life yield amazing positive results.

Day 233

"If you never experience the chill of a dark winter, it is doubtful that you will ever cherish the warmth of a bright summer's day. Nothing stimulates our appetite for the simple joys of life more than the starvation caused by sadness or desperation." – Dr. Sandra C. Duru

Sadness Can Be Inspiring - See The Bright Side Of Life.

Do you know that many of the people who appreciate their lives, health, wealth, and other good things they enjoy the most are those who have suffered and poorly struggled to have those things at all?

Sadness, loneliness, lack, and even desperation can be an inspiration at times because the pain you've experienced could motivate you to work extra hard, never to have to go through them again.

So, if you're having a bad patch and going through some sad and lonely times presently, my love, please try to look on the bright side that this experience will serve as fuel and inspiration for you someday soon.

Soon, your story, too, can become a point of reference and motivation. However, you must use all the pain and negativity you feel today and let them inspire and not demotivate you until you reach your life goals.

Day 234

"As much as it is important to pray and have wishful thinking and assertions, they are insufficient to alter your destiny and status in life if you don't devise workable strategies and tactics to actualize them." – Dr. Sandra C. Duru

You Need Strategies As Much As Prayers To Succeed In Life!

My love, one thing I've noticed in many parts of the world where religious centers are numerous and the people are deeply inclined thus is that too many go about with the wrong notion and mindset about success and even how to get it.

While it is expedient to have a relationship with your Maker and be in tune with nature, my dear, you must also know that the same nature has strict rules and ordinances it follows and obeys. Hence, you can never hit those marks and goals you're chasing if all you do is sit in one spot and pray all day.

Yes, you cannot have such a relationship or communion with God without prayer, but if that is all you do is pray alone without having any clear-cut and well-laid-out plans to achieve your dreams, you can never amount to much in life that way, my dear.

You need strategies, working plans, and a clear blueprint, not just prayers, to make it in this world. Even the Master said to "watch and pray," so why would you only focus on one and neglect the other?

Day 235

"Your future depends on what you do today, how you do it, and who you spend time with. My dear, you can't be found sitting around with people who don't have dreams, visions, or ideas daily and expect to do better."

Your Life Depends On Those You Hang Around...Literally!

As much as I'm looking for ways to put this as subtly as possible, I also can't help but acknowledge that any attempt to soften this may neutralize the message. You are who you roll with.

How do you have dreams of building one of the tallest and most magnificent skyscrapers in the world but consistently sit to discuss ideas with folks who firmly believe a 2-story duplex is too high, yet expect to keep such goals alive?

No matter how hard you try, my love, your environment rubs off on you in both positive and hugely negative ways, and this is one of such adverse instances. Never hang around people whose vision is to be purposeless and ordinary.

You were created for much greater things than mediocrity, so please watch the company you keep!

Day 236

"You are an enlightened soul, equipped with the power to design an authentic new life of happiness and fulfillment and be inspired to make a real difference in the world. Start living up to your potential today!" – Dr. Sandra C. Duru

There Is So Much You Can Yet Achieve - Live Up To Them!

One of my favorite sayings is: "To whom much is given, much is expected." I love this so much because of the way it applies to every human being God has created and placed on this planet.

Each of us is filled with so much potential and limitless power, and it gladdens my heart whenever I imagine the boundless possibilities I am yet to explore. Still, it also saddens me to see so many people living timid, caged, subdued, and troubled lives when made and given so much more!

Please, my love, always remember that no matter your situation, you have not even begun scratching the surface of what you're capable of! You can achieve so much, and many unexplored possibilities and opportunities await you; hence, you must live up to them!

All the happiness and fulfillment you could ever desire has already been placed within your grasp with all the Creator has equipped you. Don't live a substandard life!

Day 237

"No matter how long and dark your tunnel is, no matter how fierce the battle you are fighting is or how badly life has dealt with you, keep pushing, and keep holding on. Your days of rage will soon be a thing of the past." – Dr. Sandra C. Duru

No Bad Season Can Last Forever - Nothing Ever Does!

My love, have you ever been through a series of bad times that kept coming consecutively to the point where you thought you were probably trapped in a maze of ill luck?

I had an unfair share of this in 2016, and it was like the whole world was against me. However, by HIS mercies and grace, I pulled through and came out more blessed than I was when it started.

What I learned through this experience, too, though, is that you must never give the enemy reasons to rejoice over you by quitting because the going got tough. That rough season shall pass away, too, no matter how bad it looks or is, and you will come out victorious and better if you don't give up.

No bad season can last forever, my dear; nothing ever does! You will pull through this, too, so don't stop fighting, champ.

Day 238

"Keep up your mental toughness while at it, and be prepared for anything, too. The root of all human happiness is having a sense of concern for others and being good to one another." – Dr. Sandra C. Duru

Be Good To Others Always, But Never Let Your Guard Down.

Hello, my love. Do you know many people love hunting and taking advantage of good-natured and compassionate people? Sadly, it's true, and there's one way to stay ahead of them.

As much as you're a kind, humble, compassionate, and well-meaning person (which is excellent, mind you!), you must also be physically and mentally tough, too, so that the nasty comments and attempted manipulations of such people will never work on you.

I know there's a sense of joy and fulfillment in lifting others and seeing another person's life blossom because of the help you were able to render to them. However, you must also be wary of some whose delight is in spreading malicious rumors about good people, and always ensure to keep them blocked from your circle.

Yes, it's great to be good and help others, but you must never let your guard down and allow such low lives to manipulate you.

Day 239

"To complete your amazing life journey successfully, you must turn every dark tear into a pearl of wisdom and find the blessing in every battle, bad situation, mistreatment, and every curse." – Dr. Sandra C. Duru

There's A Blessing In Every Curse - Find It!

My love, has anyone ever told you that goodness is always hidden in every evil and a blessing dwelling in each curse you encounter? Hard to comprehend, right? But this is so true.

Remember when Jacob presumably lost his favorite son, Joseph, to unidentified wild beasts, and then years later, a supposed mean ruler demanded to see Joseph's younger brother, Benjamin, or he would not attend to them? That must have been a very dark period in the older man's life, but we all know how it ended in great rejoicing, victory, and testimonies, don't we?

Like Jacob and even his son Joseph had to do, my dear, learn to trust God entirely no matter what you're going through and trust that it will never end in defeat for you. There's a blessing in every curse, victory hiding in every seeming defeat, and this is the surest way to find it - by staying positive and never flinching in your trust in HIM constantly!

Day 240

"Often, the obstacles in your path can be temporary, momentary glitches. Other times, they are more complex and formidable and can threaten to delay you indefinitely. But when you do not give up on your dreams, have a direction and clear vision of your mission, and put in all the necessary actions required to succeed, you will end up feeling fulfilled in life." – Dr. Sandra C. Duru

Fulfillment Is Like Courage - It Remains Despite The Battles!

Do you know that living a fulfilled life and enjoying all of the goodness and joys of life are things you can do no matter the obstacles, battles, or challenges you face?

As courage is not the absence of fear but the refusal to bow and cave in to it, your refusal to quit and throw in the towel in the face of battles and obstacles guarantees you an eventual life of fulfillment, success, and peace.

This is why fulfillment is like courage in many ways, as it remains despite all threats to your happiness, and it is in conquering those obstacles you become the accomplished and satisfied person you've always longed to be.

So, don't give in to the frustrations, but keep pursuing your well-crafted plans, strategies, and dreams, and it will all add up and pay up for you sooner than later, my love.

Day 241

"You have to be able to objectively assess any mental roadblocks and step away from your emotions to identify a new route and keep moving forward. You must always, at all times, move forward, even if it's at a snail's pace." – Dr. Sandra C. Duru

Never Stay Stagnant By Avoiding Emotional Baggage - Keep Moving!

Are you familiar with a common saying that "slow movement is always better than no movement," my love? This is one of the most significant truths ever uttered by any man!

Another significant truth you must know and take to heart today is that emotional baggage can become mental roadblocks in your path and stop you from achieving your God-given purpose. Hence, you must rid yourself of everything that easily besets and always attacks your peace of mind.

You must never stay stagnant and keep moving along your life path by avoiding unnecessary emotional and mental drama. Be more objective and less emotive about any situation, and you will certainly never be stranded, no matter what you're up against, my dear.

Day 242

"The people who do evil things to you do everything to put negative thoughts in your head. They socially ostracize you, yet they act like the victim. The interesting part about an underminer or an oppressor is that, although they're victimizing you, they often act like the victim." – Dr. Sandra C. Duru

Stop Dancing To Society's Tunes - Don't Play Yourself For A Fool!

Have you ever had an occasion to pause one day and ponder why many people who attack, despise, and spite you do what they do? I'll share a critical reason with you today.

My dear, the most significant and ultimate aim of the enemy is to enslave and mess up your mind by consistently attacking you yet also claiming ignorance. These things are done deliberately to break you and cause you to have a mental breakdown where you begin to see and think nothing good of yourself and become very negative about everything.

Once you fall into this trap, the enemy's assignment is finished because he knows self-destruction is imminent and sure. Don't play yourself by following and dancing to society's tunes about your life, man.

No one knows you better than yourself, so keep away from such negativity and stay true to yourself always.

Day 243

"Until you learn to prioritize what matters to you, you will not be able to live a life of true happiness, abundance, peace, fulfillment, and purpose." – Dr. Sandra C. Duru

Lack Of Priorities Is A Priority...A Pretty Terrible One, Though!

My love, how are you doing today? I can't help but smile as I remember an old wise saying because it is in perfect synch with nature's voice to us today. Wisdom warns everyone, "If you fail to plan, you have already planned to fail."

However, many people still either fail or choose not to understand that we are products of our daily choices, and we must continually make the right ones to get the desired results we want for our lives.

Happiness, good health, peace, wealth, and every other good thing you seek are not impossible for you to have, but you must be disciplined and set your priorities right so that you don't keep making the wrong choices.

Having no priorities and preferences is actually a priority, too, you know, but it is awful as it means that you have prioritized failure instead of success. Please don't do that to yourself, my love!

Day 244

"Getting to the top of the rung in any sphere and endeavor requires a level of sacrifice not asked of everyone or just about anyone. The journey to true greatness and self-actualization is not a sprint but a marathon." – Dr. Sandra C. Duru

Success Is A Journey Of Years, Not Minutes - Lose The Hurry.

My beloved friend, if there is nothing you take to heart in every voice of nature you've ever come across, please don't ignore this vital one. It will save you from needless and avoidable hypertension and depression with ease.

Nobody who has ever achieved anything genuinely tangible and meaningful regarding success in life has done it overnight or in one day. Lose the hurry, my love, because success is certainly not a day's journey but one that takes years!

There is a steep price to pay for it, too, and not everyone can readily discipline themselves for such. Besides your planning and precision, you must be willing to patiently wait as you discover, develop, and build up your value through your talents, gifts, and God-given purpose.

No one hurriedly jumps into success unless they want to be a shooting star in life. I'm pretty sure you don't want that for yourself, my love, do you?

Day 245

"Determination without discipline and hard work doesn't yield good results. You must be determined to succeed yet disciplined, intentional, and consistent with a passion for your work. Nothing good comes easy." – Dr. Sandra C. Duru

Hard Work And Consistency Are Vital For A Determined Person - Don't Undo Yourself.

My love, have you ever seen anyone go to a stream, river, or tap and successfully fill a basket to the brim with water and carry it off? That would be a sight to behold, but sadly, it's impossible.

If you must fill a basket with water, you must plug all the holes tightly. This also applies to your life if you are determined to succeed but lack discipline. You must ensure that hard work and passionate consistency are never lacking in whatever you do, or else you will be like that person trying to fill a basket with water.

Stop undoing yourself by refusing to be passionately committed and putting everything into your cause, vision, dreams, and purpose, my dear.

Hard work and consistency are not optional for a determined person, as they are the key to unlocking the success you crave. So, again, my dear, please don't undo yourself by neglecting them.

Day 246

"There are things you cannot buy with material wealth. Money can't give you life or peace. Many people are ready to exchange all their money for freedom, good health, true love, happiness, and peace of mind at this time, but it is not possible." – Dr. Sandra C. Duru

There Are Many Things Money Cannot Buy - Don't Be Conceited!

My dear, the voice of nature to you today is more of a prayer than anything else, but it also encourages you to live a fruitful and edifying life.

May you never encounter and fall into problems that all your money in this world will not be able to save you from. Amen! Oh, my love, I have seen countless such cases, and they're not what I would wish even on my enemy.

Please understand that money is essential for many things and purposes, but not everything. Hence, you must never lose your direction, focus, or purpose because of it!

Never become conceited and start misbehaving toward people because of anything you have today. Life is so fleeting, and there are many things in it that your money can never buy, so you must remain humble always.

Voice Of Nature (Vol.1) By Sandra Duru

Day 247

"Trauma is like heavy baggage from the past that obstructs our progress in the present. It comes in many forms, but you can heal from those emotional wounds." – Dr. Sandra C. Duru

No Matter The Weight, You Can Let Go Of That Trauma Today - Try It!

Many things happen to us that we find almost impossible to let go of in life because of several factors. It could be the pain, regrets, humiliation, anger, or bitterness caused by such betrayals that keep us bound, but that's what they do - they bind us!

Would you jump into the deep end of a pool or river with a ship's anchor tied around your waist? Of course, you won't because you don't want to kill yourself. Sadly, though, we do this to ourselves every day that we refuse to let the baggage from those traumatic experiences go.

No matter the weight of that bad experience and how painful it is, you can heal by simply letting go from your heart and asking God and nature to help rid you of bitterness.

Life is super exciting and sweet without any needless baggage, my love. Try it today!

Day 248

"Always strive to ignite the energies in your inner mind and soul, increase your mental toughness, and increase your inner strength to keep pressing on, no matter the challenges, circumstances, or the situation you find yourself." – Dr. Sandra C. Duru

The Superhero You Need Is Inside You - Awaken It!

My dear friend, are you aware that many of the struggles you're battling against today may be because you keep ignoring the immense potential the Creator has deposited inside you?

Many times, we continue crying to others for help and keep looking outward when all we need to do is stop fretting, take a deep breath, and look inward first before anything else.

Part of this involves calling out to your Maker first and aligning yourself with all the forces of nature around you by building up your mental toughness and strength, and you'll be amazed at the things you'll begin to achieve effortlessly.

You don't need any knight in shiny armor to swoop in and rescue you, my dear. The superhero you need is inside you already, so awaken it and reap today's tremendous benefits!

Day 249

"Money does make a person happier, but only to a certain extent. When you reach a comfortable lifestyle and don't worry about your basic needs anymore, having more money doesn't bring you more happiness." – Dr. Sandra C. Duru

More Money Only Makes You Happy When You're Still Struggling - Aim Higher!

Can I ask you a question today, my love? Who would be most thrilled if you offered to give them $1,000 on the spot - a renowned billionaire or a hungry and homeless man?

This is the funny truth about money - it only excites you a lot and makes you very happy when you're still stuck or going through a level of financial lack. However, you will attain a level that even more than $1,000 will mean nothing if it isn't accompanied by things money cannot buy, like self-fulfillment and actualization.

Hence, I want to encourage you to aim higher than only meeting your physiological needs from today and start planning to be more and do more in life because you can, and you will if you put your mind to it!

Day 250

"As much as it is true that nothing lasts forever, always remember that life and success are never a straight line. There are many bumpy roads to cross. You may ask yourself: 'Am I doing the right thing? Am I good enough? Am I strong enough?' Yes, you are!" – Dr. Sandra C. Duru

Never Doubt Yourself Due To Setbacks - They're Normal!

There are so many heartbreaking things in life, but one of the worst I know is for people to completely lose their self-worth, self-esteem, and self-confidence because they've been through too many traumatic experiences.

This is truly sad, my love, but I have great news for you today; please listen to nature's voice. No matter the hardships and tribulations you get knocked down, you can never be useless, valueless, or no good!

Your situation and present circumstances do not and can never define you, so yes, dear, you are more than enough! You are loved, intelligent, brave, resilient, resourceful, and beautiful, and you not only deserve the best in life, but you will get them too!

Please always remember that setbacks and trials are a normal part of the process of your glorification in life, so you must never doubt yourself because of them. Hold on relentlessly; very soon, you will taste that sweet victory and rejoice for the rest of your days.

Day 251

"When you have difficulties, challenges, and problems, you only need to pay attention and work on them. However, when you seek attention from your problems, you start losing focus on the things that matter most." – Dr. Sandra C. Duru

In Times Of Trouble, Pay Attention, Not Seek It!

My love, has anyone ever told you that there is a clear difference between paying attention to something and seeking attention from that thing? This seemingly minor technicality can prove extremely vital many times.

Paying attention to issues, challenges, and the battles around you gives you an edge in knowing and understanding your afflictions and afflicters well enough to eventually beat them.

However, when the storms of life hit and you go about seeking attention, you become like a charity case and an object of ridicule and pity, and these are abominations before your Creator!

HE has invested and put too much inside you to become such a pitiful sight, so never fall into such, my dear, no matter what you encounter!

Day 252

"Heartbreak is an eye-opener to the darkness of the world. Heartbreak is a compulsory course in this journey through life. Heartbreak is your ladder of growth. Listen to your broken heart. Look within the cracks of your broken heart; there you will find all you seek." – Dr. Sandra C. Duru

There Is Beauty In Heartbreak...If You Observe And Listen Well!

I know that the first thing many of us do whenever we feel the intense pain that betrayals and heartbreaks cause is to fold up and recoil into ourselves. However, what if I told you your reaction is robbing you of some good in that situation, my love?

Yes, some good, I said, because contrary to what you think, heartbreaks are not complete disasters but only if you can learn to be calm enough to listen and observe closely when they occur.

Every heartbreak has a message, a vital lesson, and an opportunity to grow tremendously. Hence, you must always strive to remain calm enough to observe and not miss those critical cues from them so that you may use them as stepping stones to your next level instead of the obstacles and stumbling blocks the enemy meant them to be!

Day 253

"We have learned to hide instead of showing up in our glory. Instead of avoiding your pain, you must confront it by sitting with the emotion and loving it whenever it arises. Love alone conquers all!" – Dr. Sandra C. Duru

Nothing Else Can Overcome Pain And Hate - Embrace Love!

My beloved friend, do you know that when you react adversely to the pain and hate you receive from others, you only enable the enemy to keep adding more victims to his vicious circle of destruction?

Instead of hiding away in misery when pain strikes your heart, show up and embrace it, and more importantly, refuse to give it back. When you repay pain and hate with love, you overcome the evil the enemy meant for you and also deliver not only yourself from his terrible web but countless others after you.

So, please embrace love today, my darling.

Day 254

"Many see failure as a terrible thing, so they do everything they can never to fail, yet they do. To succeed, you must be willing to fail, be underestimated, discouraged, make mistakes, encounter challenges, be wrong, and start all over again with lessons learned from the mistakes, bad experiences, and failure." – Dr. Sandra C. Duru

When You Run From Failure, You May End Up In It - Face It Boldly!

My love, how are you today? Nature's voice speaks again about the importance of failure in our lives, and I cannot help but remember the story of Job and a vital lesson for us in it.

He said: "That which I greatly feared is come upon me," when he received the news that all he had, including all his children, had been wiped out entirely (read Job chapter 3). This clearly shows that the failure and doom we desperately seek to escape may eventually catch up because our Creator and nature abhor fear!

Never be afraid of failing or falling in life, my dear. Instead, welcome and embrace them because, through them, you will indeed become a much better, wiser, and complete individual whose capacity and abilities are beyond doubt due to the experience of going through such and coming out victorious!

Day 255

"Keeping track of what went wrong and what you got right today can help you know how to improve tomorrow. Taking notes about your daily thoughts and activities helps you keep tabs on positive growth, possible stagnancy, or unwanted retrogressions." – Dr. Sandra C. Duru

Tabs And Notes Help You Stay In Check - Keep Them!

My dear, are you aware that you must learn to take notes in both victories and defeats because there are vital lessons to learn in all situations you encounter?

Whether in victory or defeat, success or failure, keeping tabs on yourself and taking notes helps you see your flaws and strengths and obviously allows you to become a much better person in many ways.

Tabs and notes help you to stay in check, my love; hence, you must never joke with keeping them because continuous growth is paramount in every area of your life.

Day 256

"Life is fascinating, and our happiness should not be tied to material things, power, status, or money. When our ambition is grounded, it leads us to work joyfully. It also makes us comfortable, confident, happy, and our emotional well-being is guaranteed." – Dr. Sandra C. Duru

Never Tie Your Joy To Material Things - You Will Be Disappointed!

My love, have you ever been told that seeking happiness, joy, and contentment in anything your resources can buy and control is like setting yourself up for a substantial emotional fall sooner or later?

Yes, it is, because no matter how rich, powerful, affluent, and stable you may think you are, you have zero power or control over nature and anything it may decide to bring your way at any time. Only the Creator does; hence, you must seek your joy and always find your happiness in HIM alone!

This life can be an exhilarating and sweet experience for you, but only if you live and do it right. Focus on the right things; the joy you seek will never elude you.

Day 257

"You're not here to do anything perfectly; you're here to do it uniquely. Sometimes it takes many years of spiritual suffering to get us rooted in our authenticity." – Dr. Sandra C. Duru

You Are Called To Be Unique, Not Perfect - Don't Beat Yourself Up!

Hello, my love. Have you been battling with yourself and have found your self-esteem dipping lately because you've been unable to execute your plans, goals, and projects flawlessly?

Well, what if I told you that you are placing yourself under undue strain because you were not created to be perfect but unique? Yes, my dear, your primary assignment is to be like no other person on earth by ensuring that all you do is unique and never copied or forced.

Am I encouraging you to be mediocre? Far from it! However, my dear, attaining that level of perfection you rightly crave isn't a walk of a few days or projects but one of many years and practice. So, why beat yourself up about something you weren't even created to be in the first place and can only achieve through years of consistent practice?

Day 258

"Never let go of the truth because it is your savior. Always remain that strong person who is not afraid of their truths. It will not only make you free indeed, but it will also strengthen you never to give up!" – Dr. Sandra C. Duru

The Truth Is Your Anchor In Life - Hold On To It!

My love, do you know that there is so much honor, pride, and dignity in speaking the truth, no matter what you may seem to stand to lose, than siding with or telling lies and gaining the world?

Oh, yes, my dear. What does a person truly gain when they amass things through lies, deception, and falsehood? Absolutely nothing! Whatever you achieve through such a despicable manner and way of life is like building a house with no solid foundation on sinking sand. It's only a matter of time before it comes crashing down!

The truth is your savior and anchor in life; hence, you must hold fast to it and never let it go, my love.

Day 259

"You can sense when someone doesn't want you to do better than them. You can know when they want to control you. Whenever you sense these things and disposition about a person, do not hesitate to cut off and walk away immediately, no matter who or what that person may be to you" – Dr. Sandra C. Duru

Never Keep Jealous Narcissists In Your Circle - No Good Can Come From Them!

Have you ever been told that nobody can genuinely desire your growth and progress except the Creator and anyone HE sends to you? My dear, please take a closer look at the people around you today.

How many of them are genuinely happy whenever you break new ground and achieve great things? You can tell when a smile shared with you is fake or genuine, and ignoring seemingly little cues like this could prove fatal in the long run.

So, please, my love, never allow jealous, narcissistic people to remain around you, no matter the promise or purpose they seem to find around you today. Cut them off and look to your Maker alone for help! What help can an evil person even give you, if not one that would eventually turn on and destroy you?

Be wise, my dear! It is better to be safe than to be sorry, remember?

Day 260

"Always remember that pigeons flock together, but eagles fly alone. Nobody will understand your dream until it becomes a reality. Don't be afraid to go at it alone for a while until you're established." – Dr. Sandra

There Is Hardly Any Progress Running With A Crowd - Go Alone!

Do you know one fascinating thing about those who eventually win many long-distance races and marathons I've been opportune to watch? They are always determined and quick to pull away from the crowd and face their race alone.

As much as you need people to achieve your purpose in life, you must never become trapped in running with a crowd, my dear, because no great achiever ever succeeds that way. Always ensure that you're not sucked into the trends and crowd mentality this generation is so quick to align with because none can ever understand and know your purpose in life better than you.

Hence, you must never be afraid to pull out from the crowd and go at it alone. They will all flood back to celebrate with you and stay around you anyway, so why hinder yourself by flocking with them now?

Day 261

"You must find your true path and follow it diligently until you arrive at your place of purpose and rest. Nobody knows you but you. Show the world who you are!" – Dr. Sandra C. Duru

Your Success Depends On Who You Follow - The Only Leader You Need Is You.

Many times in life, we've become disoriented and confused because of the different voices, ideologies, theories, and doctrines we listen to and follow when all we need is our unique identity and path first!

Only a person who knows who they are can be confident about their destination in life. Otherwise, you will end up anywhere because you have neither found your true purpose nor connected with it, which is why many still struggle with finding their genuine rest.

The only leader you need is yourself because nobody can ever know you better. Find your purpose and stay doggedly on it, and you will achieve all your desires, my love.

Day 262

"You are created in a very unique way, and that makes you very special. You don't need anyone to complete your beautiful life because you are already complete. You have everything in you to be who you want to be." – Dr. Sandra C. Duru

The Final Piece In Your Life's Puzzle Is Already With You - Want To Know It?

My beloved, are you aware that, just as our Maker is self-sufficient and all-abiding in all things, you were also created to be complete in yourself, and you do not need any extra piece to beautify the puzzle called your life?

As much as man is a social being, my dear, you were also made in the image of your Creator, which gives you the ability to abide and flourish all by yourself if the situation warrants such.

You are an extraordinary and profoundly unique creature; all you need to excel is already in you. Find it, find yourself and a genuine purpose in life, and your flourishing will know no bounds, my love.

Day 263

"No matter what you do to prevent it, or how hard you work against such, some people will come into your life to take away everything you have worked for and leave you empty-handed and stranded if you allow them. Stay guarded always!" – Dr. Sandra C. Duru

Evil People Will Always Be Evil - Don't Break Any Sweat Over Them!

on others and making them suffer, and you also wonder what their joy and gain are in such terrible behavior, right?

Well, my dear, nature would have you know today that no matter how good you are to a scorpion, the only thing it knows is to sting and kill, and one day, it will turn on and strike you, too. Hence, you must never let your guard down around such people, especially those you've confirmed to be such devious characters!

An evil person will always be evil, my dear, so don't break any sweat over their despicable and detestable ways of living. Instead, ensure that you always protect yourself and yours from their schemes, and may God watch over you, too. Amen!

Voice Of Nature (Vol.1) By Sandra Duru

Day 264

"Your purpose is to be yourself. The full spectrum of your weirdness is what the world is waiting for. Return to your infant innocence!" – Dr. Sandra C. Duru

You Are Not Weird; You Are Unique - There's A Difference!

Have you been labeled things like weird, strange, and other odd names because you never seem to go with the crowd or conform to anybody or society's perceived norms? Here's a fascinating truth from nature to you today, my love.

No, you are not weird but certainly different from others because you are unique, and you've chosen to embrace it. This is nothing to feel bad about or be ashamed of. On the contrary, it is something to be incredibly proud of because you've discovered your true purpose and become one with it so much that others are starting to notice and label you for it.

This is the only way to stand out and achieve all you've been created to be, my dear. Hence, you must never let anyone make you feel bad about it!

Day 265

"Someone's life and destiny somewhere out there is dependent and waiting on your story to get the strength they need to break free, too. Come out of that shell and start sharing today." – Dr. Sandra C. Duru

You Didn't Survive To Hide - You Escaped To Help Others!

My love, I know that sometimes we remember everything we've been through and just want to curl up like a ball somewhere and never open up to anyone again. However, that is the enemy's plan and not your Creator's wish for you.

See, you didn't survive those betrayals, pain, embarrassments, trials, afflictions, and battles to become a frail shadow of yourself. Hell no, my dear! You escaped the enemy's clutches, so your story and testimonies can help others build the faith they need to break free.

So, please get up today and step into the limelight to start sharing your incredible story because countless lives and destinies are counting on you to survive. You won't want to let them down, now, will you?

Day 266

"It is not very hard to see when people try to limit your progress. Some people will never celebrate your achievements, but they will try hard to belittle any progress you are making. You don't need that type of energy around you." – Dr. Sandra C. Duru

Get Rid Of Negative Energies Around You - You Can't Get Far With Them!

No matter who or whatever it is some people bring to the table of your life, and your quest to achieve your dreams, negativity, hatred, jealousy, and destructive criticism are things you must never allow around you, my love.

Hence, you must cut such people off immediately after you observe these traits in them! And some of them are even bold about it because they feel like you need them and can't reach your destination without them. News flash, my dear: The only person you can never afford to lose is God. Every other person is disposable!

Please eliminate all negativity around you because you can never amount to anything good with such evil energy in your life.

Day 267

"Reconnect your spirit and soul to join the never-giving-up strong spirits already established within you to activate. The sooner you do this, the sooner you will begin healing, recovery, and your career of improvement and prosperity." – Dr. Sandra C. Duru

Activate Your Powers Within - You Are Stronger Than You Think!

My beloved, are you aware that the human body, spirit, and soul were designed and created to be self-repairing as much as they're self-sufficient, too?

This means that all you need to heal and blossom from any trials, tribulations, or afflictions are already deposited inside you, and you don't require any outside influence to get back on track in your life's journey.

Yes, my dear. You need to activate the powers your Creator and nature have endowed you with and start living up to your potential today. You are much stronger than you think, so never belittle or download your strengths again!

Day 268

"Don't ask yourself: 'What do I want to do?' Instead, ask yourself: 'Who do I want to be?' 'What do I want to do?' is focused more on a task, whereas 'Who do I want to be?' is focused more on identity or even quality of life." – Dr. Sandra C. Duru

Focus On Things That Matter - You'll Get To Your Destination Faster!

Do you know that many of us also struggle badly with achieving our dreams, goals, visions, and God-given purpose because we keep focusing on the wrong things and miss out on important ones?

My love, you have no business bothering about things that happen to you along your quest and journey to your purpose, but your aim must never leave the mark you have set for yourself.

Focus on the things that matter, and not trivial issues and things, my love, and you will assuredly get to your dreams, goals, vision, purpose, and destination in life faster than you could ever have imagined!

Day 269

"You were not made to grovel before anyone and to be trampled upon, but to reign and dominate in life as royalty because you are the child of The King of all kings! You are important, and you are unique. Never forget or lose sight of this fact!" – Dr. Sandra C. Duru

You Are Royalty - Never Grovel Before Anyone!

My love, I know that situations arise that threaten to break our spirits and crush our resolve many times in life, but the voice of nature has a question for you today.

If a tiger falls into a pit filled with black oil and gets its body dirty, does it stop being a river because its stripes are momentarily covered up? Of course, it never does, my dear; hence, you must never lose sight of who you are, no matter what you're up against!

You are royalty, and you must never tremble, kowtow, or grovel before anyone because they are not your Maker, and none can ever be as powerful and all-sufficient as HE is!

Day 270

"The secret to your success lies in your ability to make the best decisions and choices of who you allow in your inner circle. Always remember that many people want you to do well, but not as well as or even better than them." – Dr. Sandra C. Duru

Your Success And Safety In Life Depends On Your Circle - Stay Sharp!

Hello, my beloved. Are you aware that no matter how much some people around you profess their undying love, admiration, and support for you, many never want you to be better than them in anything?

Please be wise, my dear, and never forget the words of the Master Himself, who cautioned us to be "gentle as doves but wise as serpents" as we discuss daily dealings with people.

Your success, continuity, and safety depend on who you allow into your circle and those you give access to your life. Please be wise and stay sharp always, my love. Evil resides in people's hearts and is never written on their foreheads, remember?

Day 271

"Are you aware that you were created to be royalty in this life, no matter who your birth parents and family are? Adjust your crown. Reignite your passion. Remember your divinity. Rekindle your light. Stand in your truth. Reclaim your power, and take over today." – Dr. Sandra C. Duru

Never Mind Your Humble Beginnings - You Are A Divine Royalty!

My love, do you know that no matter how long a crown prince is away from the palace and his family, the day he discovers his true identity and returns to the palace, everything about his life will cease to be mediocre and poverty-stricken?

The realization leads to purposeful steps and actions, and this is what the voice of nature seeks to ignite in you today, my dear. If an earthly prince can turn his life around like that, how much more you, the child of the King of all kings?

Keep your head high and shoulders square. Your humble or rough beginnings do not matter; neither do they change who you are. Remember the child of whom you are, and begin to use that knowledge, access, and unlimited power and resources inside you to your best advantage. You were created to rule and dominate on Earth, so rise and take your place today!

Day 272

"Bad times do not last forever. It only feels like it when you're going through them because of how tough it is to endure them. But, if you learn to move forward and not move on with your grief, you will feel much better and be able to live healthily and feel great." – Dr. Sandra C.Duru

Learn To Move On Without That Bag Of Grief - You Are Loved.

My darling, are you aware that the longer those hard times persist, the more it begins to feel like there may not be a way out for you? However, I assure you today that this is the biggest lie the enemy can ever sell you, and you must not buy into it!

Nothing lasts forever, not even the good times; you will still enjoy many phases. So, why would you now believe that a bad patch and stage can endure forever because it has lasted so long?

Please do yourself a favor, my love - learn to move on without all the pain, grief, and hurt this phase may be causing you now, and never forget how much you are loved by your Creator, too.

HE promised never to leave you or forsake you, so there's no way your trials can last forever. Keep away from every negativity and continue forging ahead, and you will achieve your desired dreams sooner than later, my dear.

Day 273

"Your identity is far more than a task, job, or career. It's more so centered on purpose, vision, and mission. So, do you want to seek attention, or do you want to be the attention? What do you want to be remembered for?" – Dr. Sandra C. Duru

You Can Either Be The Follower Or The Followed - It's Your Call!

Have you ever been told that you can decide what you want to be, but even more precisely, how you want to be your heart's desire, too? This truth makes it so painful to see many people living as a shadow of the potential nature and their Creator blessed them with!

My love, you can either be followed or be a follower of one being followed by many others like you. The choice is yours, but I pray today that you will listen to this call of nature and choose the right path for yourself!

God did not create and invest this much into you to become a nonentity whose life is worse than mediocre at best but to achieve greatness and be the best at anything you set your heart upon to accomplish.

Rise today and begin to fulfill your potential, for you are far greater and more powerful than you think and give yourself credit for!

QUARTERLY SELF-APPRAISAL | REVIEW

(1) List three things you are determined not to repeat again in the last quarter of this year.

(2) What part of this quarter did you get the most things done, and what part of it did you least enjoy?

(3) Are there any skills or upgrades to your abilities that you picked up this 3rd quarter?

(4) On a scale of 1-10, rate the level of success achieved this 3rd quarter and why you think you deserve your allotted mark.

(5) How do you plan to create value with the new skills and upgrades to your abilities in the last quarter of this year?

QUARTER 4:

DAY 274 - DAY 365

Day 274

"Doubt is a medium your mind uses to draw lines on what you can achieve. Without it, the future is truly a boundless space for you to explore. Never entertain it!" – Dr. Sandra C. Duru

Doubt Is An Enemy That Cages You - Fight It Always!

My love, do you know there may not be a better description of a doubtful person and how the Creator sees and relates with them than what the Apostle James said in his letter to the early church?

He described a doubtful person as "unstable in all their ways," adding that such people should never expect to receive anything from God (see James chapter 1). Hence, nature's voice comes to you again today as a reminder and to warn you about this subtle enemy that mightily destroys.

Doubt is your enemy, my dear, because it cages, limits, and eventually robs you of all the great things you're destined to achieve. You must always do all you can to fight and keep it out of your mind so that you may enjoy and live your life to the fullest and best of your potential.

Day 275

"The only person allowed to put a lid on your potential, skill, development, growth, and success in life is the one reading this unique quote right now – yes, you!" – Dr. Sandra C. Duru

You Are Your Only Limitation - Yes, You!

My love, isn't it funny to know that whenever you give an account of how you spent your life and time here on earth, you may have nothing and no one else to blame for anything you fail at but yourself?

You are your only limitation in life, my dear; yes, you! Hence, you must keep developing and building up your mental toughness and strength so that nothing you come against in life will ever faze you.

Also, you must never allow anyone to limit your abilities or potential. The One who made you didn't give you such limits, so why should anyone else place them on you?

Day 276

"You need to start and be consistent, taking and implementing corrections to every mistake you make in the transformation process. People will talk, but if you give them enough reason, rather than criticize you, they will market you to the world." – Dr. Sandra C. Duru

Critics Are Not Always Your Enemy - Know This And Flourish.

Do you know that it is normal for you to make some mistakes while trying to transition from one phase in life to another? That's why it's called a transition, you know?

Hence, you must never be averse to criticisms of such errors because they will help you become a much better version of yourself in the long run. You need to show and prove that those criticisms are being noted and the corrections implemented, and in no time, those same people could become your most ardent supporters and fans.

Critics are not always your enemy, my love, and knowing this truth about human nature can help you flourish beyond your biggest dreams if you catch and apply it early enough in life.

Day 277

"Whenever you find yourself in a difficult situation, patience is the first skill you must activate. Hasty choices and decisions are rarely right, so you must learn to hold your peace even in the face of trials and storms." – Dr. Sandra C. Duru

The Best Time To Hold Your Peace Is When Under Pressure - Never Rush!

My darling, are you aware that there is hardly any decision you make whenever you're pressured, angry, excited, or in a tight spot that could be right? 9.5 times out of 10, such decisions are flawed because they are influenced by emotions and taken under duress.

Hence, the best decision you can ever make in such situations and conditions is to do nothing! Hold your peace, my dear, and do all you can to be patient. The patient eyes can see the nose, an old African adage says, and even nature has proven this accurate so many times already, too.

Never be in a rush to do anything, especially when you're under some pressure! The best time to hold your peace is when you're pressed and in a tight corner because any choices and decisions you make with such a calm and patient mind will be way better and have a much higher chance of being correct decisions.

Day 278

"You need to make it a priority to learn and grow daily by building positive rituals and sticking to them. The stronger you grow and become, the better your life will feel in the long run." – Dr. Sandra C. Duru

Inner Strength And Growth Are Vital - Develop Them.

My love, there are many things and challenges in life that you can easily overcome and never have to struggle against just by deliberately building and working on yourself in every area of your life.

The saying, "No knowledge is wasted," could never be more accurate, as every new thing you learn each day becomes a pillar of strength upon which you can continue to build and grow till you become a formidable force of nature to be reckoned with.

Ignorance is a terrible disease, my dear, and you must do everything you can to avoid it. Inner strength and growth are vital to your well-being and success, so you must continually chase after and focus on them.

Day 279

"Those who surrender to doubts make way for those who keep pushing to do the unthinkable. So, you either remain a coward and live in pain all your life or stand up and face your Goliath. What will it be today?" – Dr. Sandra C. Duru

You Can Either Be A Coward And Slave Or A Champion - Which Is It?

My beloved, do you know one thing about the story of David and Goliath that fascinated me the most? It is the part where the king and the entire army of Israel were quivering in fear before the Philistine before the young boy showed up.

While they chose to cower and hide away in fear before the vicious giant, the young shepherd boy decided to be a champion and banished any fears from his heart. The result? David achieved the unthinkable by slaying Goliath and beheading him with his own sword!

What trial, trouble, and challenge terrified you and everyone around you? Today, you can choose to either continue being a coward before it and its slave, or you can decide to rise and be a champion. Which would it be, my love?

Day 280

"I can't dictate how other people must behave towards me. I can't control everything that happens. How I respond to it all is what I can manage. My power lies in my response." – Dr. Sandra C. Duru

You Always Have Power Over Your Responses - Don't Be Baited!

Hello, my dear friend. Are you aware that there is absolutely no way you can ever control or determine everything that will happen to you in life, but you can surely regulate how you react to them?

Many times, toxic people around you try to deliberately push you over the edge to provoke you into anger, but you should never fall into their traps.

While you may not have control over their evil, toxic, and narcissistic actions, you always have control and power over your reactions to their attacks, so you must never take their bait!

Day 281

> *"Peace does not mean being in a space where uncertainty, trouble, or tough realities can't exist. Peace means being in the middle of all these things and being concentrated mentally, emotionally, and physically."–* Dr. Sandra C. Duru

Peace Is Not The Absence Of War - It Abides Regardless.

My love, do you know peace and troubles can coexist in the same space as long as you precisely balance your priorities and expectations?

Yes, my dear, because "peace" cannot exist without conflict or war, but the ability to remain calm, composed, unfazed, and focused through them all makes it even more blissful!

Peace is not the absence of war but the ability to maintain a sound mind and serene physical composure because it abides regardless of the troubles, trials, and storms.

Train your mind to be at rest always, no matter the raging storms, and you're one step closer to a peaceful life than you know.

Voice Of Nature (Vol.1) By Sandra Duru

Day 282

"You are allowed to grow and even outgrow yourself! As you wake up, your daily target must be to ensure there is never a better yesterday. This applies to everything you do and every area of your daily life, including work, business, relationships, marriage, family, etc." – Dr. Sandra C. Duru

You Must Outdo Yourself Daily - No Better Yesterdays!

There are only about two other persons you're constantly competing against in your life, and they are the person you were yesterday and the version of you alive and awake today, my love.

The one awake today because every minute of that new day must be dedicated to getting better than you were some minutes back. And, of course, the person you were the previous day because there must never be a better yesterday in your life, ever!

Your life must be like the Biblical "path of the just which shines brighter and brighter on to a perfect day," and it must be so in everything concerning you, my love. Also, don't limit yourself to anything in any way, and you must never stop testing and stretching yourself daily.

This is what champions and gods are created and forged from, and you are certainly one, oh child of the Most High!

Day 283

"Patience is not about waiting for a miracle to happen; it's about keeping a good attitude while working hard on your dreams." – Dr. Sandra C. Duru

It's Not About Waiting, But How You Wait - Be Positive!

My love, are you aware that you may be praying and desperately waiting for an answer to your prayers from God, yet be the reason those prayers remain unanswered? Yes, it's possible, and here's why.

When you claim to have faith or believe in God, and you've prayed to HIM about your situation, but you still talk ill and negatively about your hopes, dreams, vision, and purpose in life, what exactly are you waiting for?

Such a person will eventually turn on God because they lack the maturity and attitude to receive HIS blessings. See, my dear, it's not about waiting but how you wait.

You cannot claim to be always waiting on God and exhibiting a chronic lack of faith and negativity. You must remain patient and positive always!

Day 284

"Anyone who tells you that you can't achieve your dream has once succumbed to his own doubt of achieving that dream. Your case will be different because you will use a different approach, so don't fret or worry." – Dr. Sandra C. Duru

Only Failures Tell You "It's Impossible" - Be Careful Who You Listen To!

If one thing is as sure as sunset and sunrise in this world, my love, it is the truth that no one can give what they don't have; hence, a person accustomed to failure can never encourage you to succeed because he doesn't know how!

Watch the people in and around your life, my love, and observe their words and actions toward any project they know you're embarking on. Please beware of the spirit and tongue that is always negative because such people breed others like themselves.

It's only a failure that will tell you that anything is impossible in this life because they have given up on success themselves. Hence you must be very careful who you listen to and take advice from!

Day 285

"If I can bring a smile to someone's face this morning, I will do it regardless of what I am going through right now. Kindness does not cost a thing!" – Dr. Sandra C. Duru

It Doesn't Take Anything To Make Others Smile - Be Humane.

My love, do you know that some of the most selfless people you've ever heard about, read of, or seen in this world are those who also have severe problems and challenges in their lives, yet they never stop giving?

That's because it doesn't take or cost anything to make others smile and be happy in this world. All you need is a genuinely loving, humble, and humane heart filled with empathy, and people will be blessed anywhere you go.

Sacrificing for others doesn't make you a fool or weak. Instead, it shows how much you're in tune with your Creator and nature, and HE will ensure that you never lack anything good because of this. Try it today!

Day 286

"Material things should not matter to you. What should matter the most is how you have lived, what you have learned, and who you have become." – Dr. Sandra C. Duru

Your Possessions And Wealth Are Immaterial - How Are You Living?

Dear friend, have you ever been to the funeral of a very wealthy person, either a long time ago or even in the recent past? You should have noticed one thing during the ceremony if you were paying attention to things that matter.

It is a fact that, no matter how affluent and influential a person is, they will never get beyond six feet when their grave is being measured and dug, regardless of the quality of their casket.

So, what manner of person do you now ought to be, and what type of life are you supposed to be living today? These are nature's questions to you, my love, and you will do well to answer them honestly and fix up sincerely if your answers are negative.

All you have acquired in this world does not matter as much as how you live. Shape up and make a positive impact on someone today!

Day 287

"Challenges would always come that would try to make you lose control of the situations you find yourself in, but how you go through them largely depends on what is going through your head. Think right always!" – Dr. Sandra C. Duru

Your Mind Must Always Be Right Else You Lose The Fight - Think Right!

My love, no matter how many times we talk about the issue of having a sound mind, many people still struggle with keeping their thoughts in line and controlling their emotions.

Hence, it is imperative that the voice of nature keeps hammering it into our ears and minds because a battle lost in the mind is a guaranteed physical loss already, and you don't want to be a constant loser, do you?

Your mind must always be right, or else you will lose the fight, and the only way to do this is to think positively and build up your mental toughness! Nothing good comes easy, so you must be ready to take on any challenges and trials head-on and never yield until you emerge victorious.

This is your surest way to victory, and you will achieve your purpose if you imbibe and master this philosophy of life.

Day 288

"Stay with your mind focused on your vision and remain confident in the pursuit of your dreams. The challenges you see or encounter are part of the building process to actualizing your dreams." – Dr. Sandra C. Duru

What Do You Call Those Battles And Challenges Before You?

Whenever you're faced with a seemingly colossal trial, challenge, or battle, what do you call and how do you see them, my love? Are they harmful obstacles to you or great opportunities for growth and better testimonies?

While some are moaning about their conditions and harsh circumstances, do you realize that many others are in that same economy and crisis, making it big time and prospering almost effortlessly?

Again, I ask you today, my dear, do you see those challenges as obstacles that will derail you or as stepping stones to your glory? What you see and say is what you get; hence, your focus must never shift from your God-given purpose, and you must never doubt your ability to achieve it no matter what stands against you!

Day 289

"Doubt is the parent of fear and worry. Rest assured that you will also witness fear and worry once you begin to tow this path. And that can never take you anywhere good." – Dr. Sandra C. Duru

Worry And Fear Always Partner With Doubt To Stop You - Boot Them Out!

There are very few types of people that the Almighty God said HE would never have anything to do with in HIS sacred word. Do you know that a person always filled with doubt is one of them, my love?

Faith is the opposite of doubt, as course and boldness are the opposite of fear, and HIS word says that without faith, it is impossible to please HIM, let alone receive anything from HIM.

What's worse is that worry and fear are always in collaboration with doubt, and once they take hold of any mind, their only plan is to ruin such and destroy everything good it has going on.

Boot them out and away from you today, my dear, and your life will experience peace, fruitfulness, and rest like never before! You deserve such things, don't you?

Day 290

"Nothing good comes easy in life, and the only things that the enemy attacks are those they already know will blossom, flourish, and prosper if they don't try to destroy it before it even buds. You are a gem. Don't give up on yourself." – Dr. Sandra C. Duru

Rejoice When The Enemy Attacks You - It Proves Your Worth!

My darling, are you aware that thieves, pirates, and bandits never attack an empty vessel or house? No, they do not because the only mission of the enemy is "to steal, to kill, and to destroy," so why bother with an empty vessel, house, or life?

Rejoice when the enemy constantly torments, afflicts, and attacks you, my dear, because these actions are more than enough proof that you are precious and loaded beyond even your imagination!

Keep forging ahead despite all you're battling through today, and you will get to your destined place of glory and rest sooner rather than later. All you have to overcome these trials are in you already, so never quit or even think of throwing in the towel because you were created to dominate and succeed, and you surely will if you don't give up!

Day 291

> *"If your parents were poor and you were born into a low-income family, it's neither your fault nor that of your parents. However, how you turn out in life is not beyond your control, and the result will be your fault entirely."* – Dr. Sandra C. Duru

What You Do With Your Life Is Your Fault - Not Your Birth Conditions!

One thing I love about my African roots and heritage is the privilege it has given me to experience so many "grass to grace" stories firsthand and to see that the Creator is yet in the business of changing destinies!

So, my love, please stop allowing that evil voice trying to keep you limited and tied down in mediocrity and poverty to rule your mind. God has made and given you so much more than meets the eyes, but you must diligently work towards unleashing those blessings and walking fully in them!

Even from all we see in nature daily, you can already tell that what you do with your life and whatever you eventually become is your fault. At this stage, you no longer have the luxury of blaming your birth conditions, humble beginnings, or poor parents.

Yes, you were born that way, but what have you done with your life ever since? That's what counts on the day of reckoning, my dear friend!!

Day 292

"Pursue your dreams like your life, and everything depends on it. Do not entertain fears or doubt. Let nobody discourage you." – Dr. Sandra C. Duru

Success Is A Do-Or-Die Matter - Yes, Treat It As Such!

Have you ever tried to examine the lives of specific individuals who have risen to worldwide prominence and acclaim in different sectors of the world's economy from practically nothing? They are people with the same mindset regarding success in life, my love.

They firmly believed there was never another option besides becoming successful in life. To them, you either "get rich or die trying," as extreme as that may sound, it propelled them to their purposes and destined glory in life.

See, my dear, until you begin to see success as a do-or-die affair and start treating it as such, you may find yourself still entertaining petty fears and doubts! Never allow any discouragements to come near you - not even from yourself!

The only line you must never cross is into a life of crime and nefarious activities in the name of hunting for success. Nothing good comes out of amassing anything in such an evil manner; hence, you must never be enticed into such an empty and naturally cursed life, my beloved.

Day 293

"One of the best ways to grow as a good leader is by learning from people you admire and not constantly complaining about situations, but giving your best in difficult times to adjust smartly for excellent results." – Dr. Sandra C. Duru

Complaints Alone Don't Solve Problems - Stop It!

Do you know that one of the worst things you can ever do to yourself is always to whine and complain about everything instead of calmly paying attention to things and people around you so you can learn and improve your situation and life?

Yes, my love. Complaints and nagging about problems don't ever solve them. Instead, they even add to the issues on the ground and further complicate matters, which is unhealthy and unproductive.

Listen to nature's voice to you today, and stop complaining instead of making intelligent contributions and doing your best to ensure things get better.

Whether in your business, marriage, relationships, social life, or even your walk with God, adopt the habit of learning instead of complaining, and you will become a certified and unstoppable achiever in all your endeavors.

Day 294

"Making ambiguous demands and not properly clarifying what your vision is all about will most often lead to a misinterpretation and errors on the part of those who may be trying to work with you to actualize it. Ensure your vision is clearly defined and spelled out." – Dr. Sandra C. Duru

State Your Objectives And Goals Clearly - Don't Confuse Your Helpers!

My love, are you aware that not clarifying even seemingly tiny details about your dreams, vision, and God-given purpose can cost you dearly in ways you never imagined it could? Yes, it can, but here's a little tip on escaping this.

You must avoid all ambiguities in anything you do. Always ensure that your objectives and goals are perfectly stated or well documented so that your helpers may not become confused instead of being convinced about your vision and motivated to sponsor or assist you.

Even the good book says to "write the vision and make it plain, that he may run with it that readeth it," remember? The key word here, and nature's voice today, is that you must state your dreams and purpose clearly, so please learn and keep to this simple rule, and you will find the help and comfort you need to actualize your vision.

Day 295

"Your attitude towards wealth building or creation will determine how well you can handle economic security and sustainability. This is the best kind of financial legacy to leave. Money is wonderful, but attitude is everything." – Dr. Sandra C. Duru

Attitude Determines Who Stays Rich Or Goes Bankrupt - Watch Yours Always!

There are quite a few things that can control the type of wealth both nature and the Creator would eventually decide to release into your hands as a person, and one of such is your attitude, especially towards economic matters, my love.

Money is always attracted to those who know how to use, manage, and control it well; hence, the rich keep getting richer, and the poor get poorer. If you must chase anything with all your might right now, get enough financial literacy and discipline first!

Attitude determines who goes bankrupt or who stays rich in life, and this knowledge will not only help you know how to create wealth but how to retain it as well - which is equally, if not even more important, I dare say, my love.

Day 296

"Education is not a privilege but a necessity. It is equally as important as the air we breathe, the food we eat, and our right to livelihood. In fact, education can be considered food for the mind too." – Dr. Sandra C. Duru

An Ignorant Mind Is A Liability To You - Get Educated.

As many people may not fully realize the depth of what education does to the human mind, you cannot afford to be ignorant of or downplay it, too, my love.

An ignorant and uneducated mind is a liability and more of a plague to its owner because it remains short-sighted, uninformed, primitive, and many other things that are detrimental to the dreams and purpose of anyone.

Hence, you must understand that getting educated is not a privilege but a compulsory need that must be duly satisfied by all means necessary! Oh, and I hope you know this is also not restricted to the walls of any formal learning institution, don't you?

You can educate your mind by reading voraciously and taping into every opportunity to learn something new. Your mind needs to be developed and adequately groomed, and you must see to this because it is for your good, my dear.

Day 297

"Your passion and drive over your dreams and vision is an infectious thing that can easily spread to those within your circle when you believe and pursue it passionately." – Dr. Sandra C. Duru

Don't Bother About Followers - Your Passion Will Infect Them!

My love, do you know that it's totally out of line for you to actively seek people to believe in your dreams, goals, and visions because it is like placing the cart before the horse as you try to ride along?

All you need to gain the followers, fans, and supporters you require for your dream is inside you already, and it is the amount of passion, dedication, determination, and zeal they see you put into it that will attract and bring them.

Stop chasing after people when they ought to be running after you! Dedicate and give yourself wholly to your craft, and in no time, you will have the whole world at your doorstep celebrating, hailing, and chanting your name as a successful icon!

Day 298

"You may have been born into a poor and humble beginning, but you can either remain poor or work yourself and your family out of poverty. There is no limit to what you can achieve in every area of your life once your mind is made up to do it." – Dr. Sandra C. Duru

Poverty Doesn't Limit You. Your Mind Does. Liberate It!

My beloved, are you aware that if a person's mind is unlearned, undisciplined, financially illiterate, and poverty-stricken, they will surely be back to being worse than broke and bankrupt in a little while if you gave them $1 billion?

That's because poverty is the state of your mind and not what you have in your pocket or bank accounts! This is why a person born into an impoverished family can grow into a wealthy magnate and rescue his lineage from poverty if their mind is right because they'll understand that it's their choice to either remain wretched or become rich in life.

Poverty doesn't and has never limited anyone in this world, my love; your mind does. Hence, you must liberate your mind and ensure that it is not limited or ignorant from today.

Day 299

"One of the strongest oppositions that the enemy will raise against you is the feeling of despair as you approach every new phase of your journey. However, you must never fail to remember that you started from somewhere with nothing and have already come far. Keep pushing!" – Dr. Sandra C. Duru

Every New Phase Brings Its Own Challenges - Don't Be Fazed!

Are you aware that every new phase and chapter in your life will always come with different battles, obstacles, and challenges, which are just nature's usual way of preparing and strengthening you for the journeys yet ahead?

Learn to see every battle as an opportunity to grow and enlarge your coast richly because they are, and you must never be fazed by them, no matter what!

The enemy will always use the fear of the unknown to lure your heart into despair and doubt, but you should never fall for such cheap tricks again. There is nothing ahead that you haven't conquered worse behind, and the God who brought you this far didn't do so to abandon you now, did HE?

Keep fighting and pressing on, and never relent, my love. Your success and victory are assured!

Day 300

"Hard work is the fuel you need to pump into your goals, visions, and ideas. If you are good at identifying opportunities and keying into them intentionally and smartly, you'll become successful, financially stable, and independent." – Dr. Sandra C. Duru

Opportunities Are One Thing, But Identifying Them Is Also Crucial.

My love, do you know that there are diverse opportunities around you every day that you are yet to recognize, let alone tap into? This is how the world has always been, and it's not about to change anytime soon, either.

Nature always surrounds us with enough goodness, blessings, and opportunities to thrive and live a good life. However, opportunities are one thing, but recognizing and having the skill to grab and utilize them is as crucial as having them!

Learn to spot gems even while they're yet unpolished. This is the difference between the wealthy and the poor in this world, and such an ability will aid your diligence and hard work and help you attain that level of financial independence and stability you deeply crave, my dear.

Day 301

"Start creating better goals. Stop looking for validation. Start living your dreams. Stop looking for a mentor. Start building your expertise. Stop blocking yourself, and do the right things to achieve your goals."
– Dr. Sandra C. Duru

Create Your Ideal World - You Need No Validation!

The advent of social media, all its platforms, and the boundless opportunities they opened up for people worldwide have been a blessing for everyone. Still, their terrible side effects have also not gone unnoticed recently.

Have you wondered why the rate of depression, suicide, and related evils has been sky-rocketing and keeps shooting up these days? There is greater access to people and strangers from any part of the globe, yet people are becoming depressed and feeling lonelier than ever, and the answer is pretty simple. Social media isn't so social after all!

Many have abused the privileges and access it availed the world; hence what was meant to be a tremendous life-changing tool has become a life-wrecking tool, depending on how you use it.

Nature's voice to you today urges you to create your special world and never live or seek anyone's validation; talk more strangers you hardly genuinely know on the internet!

Start doing the right things, living right, and focusing on your God-given purpose, my love, and your life will turn out perfectly in the long run.

Day 302

> "There is no harm or sin in being quick in life, but there is everything wrong with being in a hurry. You can be quick with how you do things and pursue your goals, but you should never be in a hurry!" – Dr. Sandra C. Duru

Impatience Blinds And Kills - Stay Calm Always.

Do you know that many of the things most of us rush and are always in such a hurry to do and achieve are things that would naturally happen at their appointed time if only we patiently do the right things and wait?

My love, the Creator has a plan for everyone HE made, including you and me. Hence, you should know and rest assured that no matter the obstacles and trials you face today, your time and season of joy and success, too, will come as long as you stay on the right path.

Never be in a hurry to achieve anything because such impatience will blind you and eventually kill you, leading you down dark and wrong paths that will consume you. You don't want to end up like that, do you?

Day 303

"Many times, people throw in the towel at their scripting and planning phase because they share those scripts and plans with the wrong people who kill it, or they become overwhelmed by the magnitude of their vision and start questioning their own abilities." – Dr. Sandra C. Duru

Never Doubt Your Dreams And Vision - You Are Capable!

My love, I know that there are some visions, dreams, and projects that we envisage in our minds sometimes, and almost immediately, we allow self-doubt and other negativities to set in due to the magnitude of those visions. This is so wrong, though, and you must never allow that in your mind again.

You are more than capable, my dear, and you should never doubt your ability to bring those dreams and visions to fruition. If you could not deliver them, the Creator would never have given them to you. HE never makes mistakes!

Also, you must be wary of who you share those dreams with, especially at this conception stage, because many evil people will kill it right there by sowing seeds of negativity, failure, and doubt in your mind and spirit.

Be wise, diligent, and steadfast in your faith; no dream, goal, or vision shall ever be impossible to actualize.

Day 304

"Many think leadership is about position, title, or rank; leadership is not about a title or designation. It's about impact, influence, and inspiration. Impact involves getting results, while influence spreads your passion for your work for excellent results and outstanding performance." – Dr. Sandra C. Duru

Dear Leader, How Many Lives Have You Directly Impacted?

One of the most misunderstood and misconstrued terms and concepts in all of nature is the concept of leadership and what it entails, and I want you to escape such misconceptions today, my love.

Anyone can be a leader because it is not about titles, positions, or entitlements. Instead, it is about impact, adding value to others, and being the voice of calm, reason, and strength for those with no anchor to hold them down! This is authentic leadership, my dear; hence, anyone with the proper virtues can be a leader in their space.

Stop waiting for an official assignment or office to assume this role nature bestows on its finest. And, if you do happen to hold an official office presently, ask yourself this question: How many lives have I directly impacted, improved, and established positively in my role?

The honest answers to this question will show you the way if you are truthful to yourself and others around you, and it will help you become the best leader any would desire to have.

Voice Of Nature (Vol.1) By Sandra Duru

Day 305

"The root of all evil is the love and worship of money, and those who do not check their excesses and impulses as they chase their set goals and dreams will always end up in that trap." – Dr. Sandra C. Duru

Mammon Is Like The Grave - Don't End Up In Its Claws!

My love, do you know there is a thin line between honestly desiring to be financially secure and being a greedy grabber of money?

That unquenchable thirst and longing to keep amassing money and stockpiling it, even to the detriment of everyone else around you, clearly indicates that the god of money has wrapped its arms of greed and avarice over such a person.

Never be caught in the evil claws of Mammon because, like the grave, it never says enough! Always keep your thirst and quest for monetary gains in check, and never take what you know is not rightfully yours, no matter how little!

The root of evil is the worship and excessive craze to keep grabbing money, and you would do well to avoid getting sucked into it, my best friend.

Day 306

"Gender has nothing to do with wisdom, success, knowledge, integrity, intelligence, and intellectual abilities. Men and women should be treated equally with respect and utmost importance." – Dr. Sandra C. Duru

Wisdom Is No Respecter Of Persons Or Gender - Don't Discriminate!

Among the many things I have always been deeply grateful to God our Maker for, the fact that there is no disparity between males and females when it comes to the sharing and acquisition of wisdom is topmost on my list.

Are you aware that treating someone specially because of their gender, and maltreating another over the same is the height of ignorant insensitivity and shows an appalling lack of tact?

There is nothing a person cannot achieve regardless of their gender, and discriminating against anyone when nature and the Creator apparently did not is just plain stupidity on the part of those who engage in such.

Wisdom, knowledge, wealth, intelligence, and all of nature's other goodness are no respecters of gender, so you must never discriminate against any!

Day 307

"Exceptional situations call for exceptional measures. The primary responsibility for dealing with crisis lies with us, and we must assume it fully." – Dr. Sandra C. Duru

No Crisis Is Beyond You - Step Up And Take Charge!

Are you familiar with one of the sweetest promises of God to us in HIS word? Let me share this beautiful assurance with you today, even as nature's voice comes again to edify you.

God says: "There hath no temptation taken you but such as is common to man: but God is faithful, who will not suffer you to be tempted above that ye are able; but will with the temptation also make a way to escape, that ye may be able to bear it." - 1 Corinthians 10:13.

My beloved friend, not only will HE not let the trials and temptations be greater than you, but HE will also make a way out for you. Why would you now ever choose to cower before any obstacles or fret because of any opposition or trials in life?

Step up and take charge, my dear, because no crisis is beyond your capacity! You already have all you need to excel and conquer inside you, so stop fretting and take your rightful place of authority today.

Day 308

"There is a thin line between being a leader and being a boss, ruler, authoritarian, and dictator. A boss says, 'Go and make sure you do it,' while a leader says "Let's go and make it happen." – Dr. Sandra C. Duru

Be Careful Not To Become A Dictator Instead Of A Leader - It's Pretty Easy!

Do you know it is much easier to become a version of a dictator and evil authoritarian many of us criticize and hate without knowing we have crossed the line? Yes, it is, my love, and this is how.

How do you direct, treat, relate with, interact with, and coordinate the people you have around you - whether at your place of work, home, business, school, or wherever? Putting people to tasks you would never lift a finger to help with and ordering them around till they get it done are the first traces and symptoms of this authoritarian syndrome, and it's a pitiful state.

Becoming a dictator instead of a leader is pretty easy, so you must always be on your guard against such traits and be very careful, my dear.

Day 309

"Staying true to principle is a matter of uprightness and self-respect. It includes standing up for your ethics and not caving in to the demands or prospects of others." – Dr. Sandra C. Duru

It Takes A Lot To Be A Person Of Integrity But It's Not Impossible!

My love, in a world where there seems to be little regard for virtues like honor, dignity, and integrity anymore, I know it is pretty hard to maintain these standards, but here's nature's good news for you: It is not impossible!

You only have to decide whether to retain your honor and what it's worth or debase and demean yourself by becoming like others with zero values, integrity, and scruples.

Please, my dear, you are way better and deserve much better than such a purposeless and vain life; hence, you must do everything to avoid it!

Day 310

"Waiting and following due process might seem slow and challenging, but this challenge brings out the best in you and the worst. How you attend to it defines your leadership potential." – Dr. Sandra C. Duru

How You Handle Challenges, Define Your Personality - Don't Crack.

My dear friend, do you know that no matter what you do to gold and other precious stones in a furnace, as long as the temperature is not set to a melting point, they will only continue to glow in the flames while the fire licks up every other particle around them?

And, just as fire purifies and purges precious stones, challenges, and afflictions are also nature's way of proving what stuff you are made of. You are unfit for the top if you crack and lose your way under pressure.

However, if you remain composed, continue following due process, and keep doing the right things, your leadership and outstanding personal qualities will shine through for all to see, and you will be exalted in no time.

Day 311

> "I prefer people who stick to their principles, values, and truth than those whose principles are affected by the actions of others. Always be true to yourself!" – Dr. Sandra C. Duru

Don't Be A "Yes Man" - It Is Pretty Terrible!

Do you know that one of the most significant factors to always look out for in anyone you plan to get involved with is their ability to take a stand based on their beliefs and convictions and never waver, no matter the pressure?

Whether it is a personal, business, or platonic relationship, always ensure that anyone you bring into your space can think for themselves and is not easily influenced and swayed by other people's opinions.

You must not agree with everyone you meet, my dear, and every school of thought and opinion mustn't be acceptable to you. Never be a "yes man" with no stand, conviction, or bearing! It is a pretty terrible character, and no one who wants anything concrete will ever take you seriously.

Day 312

"The goal is to be a better version of you today than you were yesterday. Don't lose sight of that, and keep drawing inspiration from any and everything around you today and always." – Dr. Sandra C. Duru

Nature Abounds With Inspiration - You Can Be Better Daily!

My love, if there is one lofty goal you should set for yourself and doggedly pursue daily with all you have, it is never to be worse today than you were yesterday in any area of your life!

The truth is that there is even no reason why you shouldn't keep improving daily because everything you need to grow and flourish has been provided for you already. I say this consistently because it is the undiluted truth, my dear.

All the resources, inspiration, guidance, and motivation you could ever need to keep improving abound in nature's splendor all around you. Learn to tap into it and become one with it, and you will be unstoppable in life!

Day 313

"A leader does not distinguish himself when everything is going well. You distinguish yourself when things are rough and tough, and you proffer solutions. This is how a great leader is identified." – Dr. Sandra C. Duru

Adversity Reveals Who A True Leader Is, Not Comfort.

Are you aware that nothing makes a leader more respectable and accepted by his people and all others around them than how they handle themselves in adversity, tribulations, and trying times?

The world is always watching, my dear; hence, you cannot afford to have a bad day in the office, especially when others look up to you for guidance.

Yes, your humanity can occasionally surface, but such a show of frailty and weakness must never become a regular feature. Adversity reveals who a great leader is, not comfort; hence, you must always be ready and willing to embrace it!

Day 314

"Our problems as a global community can only change without when we all change within – Be your brother's keeper!" – Dr. Sandra C. Duru

The Change We Desire Is With Us...It Is Us!

My love, I firmly believe that nature has said all it can and should to many of us about this particular issue, yet we virtually refuse to heed its call and warning. So, it again calls to you today.

There can hardly ever be any meaningful change without when there has been none within because it all begins from our hearts and minds before they become the actions we can see and measure.

Until we decide to only do to others as we would have them do to us and determine to be the change we desire to see in others first, many of our collective battles and challenges will continue to linger, and sadly so.

The change we desperately desire is already with us, my dear, because it is us! Wake up from your slumber, and choose to be a better person today.

Day 315

"Being true to principle can lead to liberation, self-confidence, bliss, and an ability to steer through life more efficiently. It can also lead to a sense of contentment that you've given your best to the world." – Dr. Sandra

Stay True To Your Convictions And Policies - You'll Be Glad You Did.

Do you know that the people who live the most fulfilled and satisfied lives never flinch, worry, or bulge when and if it seems the whole world is against them because of their faith and convictions?

Yes, my dear. Many such people retire to their graves with satisfied smiles because they know they lived well and stood for everything they believed in until the end.

Wouldn't you also want to experience such exhilaration and immense satisfaction even while you live because you know you're not a conformist to whims and strange doctrines blowing around you?

Stay true to your ideologies, beliefs, faith, and convictions, my dear, and I assure you that you will be super glad that you did in the long run.

Day 316

"The act of leading is an art. A leader must understand and empathize and be willing to work with others. This is what makes you a leader." – Dr. Sandra C. Duru

What Makes You A True Leader? What Does Nature Say?

My dear friend, are you aware that without a large heart filled with love, compassion, support, and empathy for others, you can never be regarded as a good, talk more a great leader?

A leader isn't one who can dish out the harshest orders and commands or who commands the most fear in those around them. Instead, they're the ones every other person naturally gravitates to in their times of trouble because they know their plight will be alleviated and their pain soothed.

A true leader is one who not only works well with others but is also the glue that holds everyone else together in more ways than can be counted! Be a great leader for others around you today.

Day 317

"You still have life; make good use of it. Dedicate to improving yourself best so that other people's lives can be turned around by your lifestyle and what you stand for." – Dr. Sandra C. Duru

Let Your Life Inspire And Help Others - What Are You Living For?

Do you know that some people would die right now, and nobody would mourn or weep over them at all, yet there are others whose death can throw an entire country into painful mourning?

Before you think it's probably because one was wealthy and generous and the other was not, I would have you know that you don't need money or influence to be a great person who all would love.

Consciously decide to ensure that your life will be an inspiration and help to others today, and whether anyone appreciates you or not, please know you're on the right path, and you must never relent! Let your lifestyle and philosophies be a stepping stone for others around you, not a stumbling block, and you're halfway there.

Day 318

"Do not be blinded by your tears to the point where you do not see the lessons in that situation because they surely exist. Life is a teacher...learn from it!" – Dr. Sandra C. Duru

Never Miss The Opportunity To Learn From Your Mistakes - Be Strong!

My love, if you think that making mistakes and having several shortcomings are tough enough to swallow, what would you now say to be in a situation where you keep repeating those mistakes because you didn't learn from them?

The worst thing that could ever happen to you is to keep falling at the same spot repeatedly; hence, you must keep your eyes open and learn from every shortcoming you suffer.

Yes, you can and should even mourn your defeats, but you must never allow your momentary sorrow to cloud your judgment and sight to the point where you don't see all you need to learn from those mistakes and life lessons.

Day 319

"Provocate yourself to be great. It takes determination and the inner power that you possess. If you want something enough, are you prepared to pay the price in your efforts to train and teach yourself to that end? Sure, you can do it!" – Dr. Sandra C. Duru

If You Are Willing To Pay The Price, You Can Have It - Push Yourself!

Are you aware that there is nothing in this world you cannot have or accomplish as long as you know what it takes and are willing and able to pay the price for it? You are your only lid, my love!

Yes, nothing and no one else can stop you when you want something bad enough, and you're willing to go all out for it. Nature's voice and truth to you today is pretty direct and simple, my dear: You can surely have it if you're willing to pay the price, so you must continually push yourself!

Day 320

"You were created and born without limitations to your greatness and abilities. Start living like the champion and achiever you are, no matter your gender!" – Dr. Sandra C. Duru

There Is A Massive Champion Inside You - Activate Your Powers!

My beloved, the voice of nature calls out to you softly again today, and it seeks to remind you of a fundamental truth: The Creator placed absolutely zero limits on your possibilities, abilities, and greatness when HE made you!

No matter how often you hear this, if you don't believe it, take it to heart and begin to function with the realization it will sadly never do you any good. My dear, there is a massive champion inside you whose abilities are limitless in ways that words cannot describe.

However, until you discover and believe in yourself that much, this unlimited power dormant inside you will sadly remain unactivated. It's totally up to you, my love, so what do you want to do with this inherent greatness today?

Day 321

"It is important for us to understand the uniqueness in our diversities as a people. We must understand that we were created differently and, by so doing, have our unique abilities." – Dr. Sandra C. Duru

There Is Beauty In Our Diversity - It Makes Life Interesting!

My beautiful friend, have you ever thought about how life would be if we all looked, thought, talked, walked, and acted the same in everything regarding us? That thought makes you cringe right now, doesn't it?

Well, what if I told you that this is, unfortunately, what you do anytime you keep trying to follow a trend, change yourself to suit a narrative, or become something other than your created nature?

Your abilities are unique, just as mine are, too, and it is in this diversity that the beauty of our human nature is displayed as we all coexist and relate daily. There is great beauty in our diversities, and this life would be unbearably boring if it weren't so. Hence, you must understand and embrace it wholeheartedly, my love.

Day 322

"We are faced with a lot of obstacles in life, but to get what you desire, you must be willing to walk alone and believe in yourself when no one does and also learn to fuel yourself with an uncommon vision while developing a rare belief in yourself." – Dr. Sandra C. Duru

Develop That Indestructible Believe In Yourself - You Are Perfect!

Life and human history have more than enough records and testimonies of people who have dared to brave it and stand against the odds, the entire world, and even the logical science of their time!

Why would two brothers doggedly refuse that man isn't restricted from flying and go ahead to invent a machine that eventually dispelled that prior fact even against all the tribulations, ridicule, and obstacles they had to face?

It's simply because they believed in themselves and their vision so much; they felt like life wasn't worth living without it, so they were willing to lay down their lives for it. You are perfect, and your dreams are valid, too; hence, you must develop that indestructible and unparalleled belief, confidence, and faith in yourself, my love!

Day 323

"Life is full of lessons, and we learn daily from good or bad experiences. If we think deeply, we will discover it is to bring out our best." – Dr. Sandra C. Duru

There Are Daily Lessons You Must Get From Life - Love Them!

Hello, my darling. I'm pretty sure that you already know by now that nothing just happens in this life and that everything nature and life throws at you is for a purpose and even for some specific reasons most times.

However, do you know that you should never be weary of receiving these lessons as they come daily, no matter what they are, because therein lays the keys to your desired growth and success?

Nothing grows out of the earth without dying first when planted, and for humankind, you must endure and overcome diverse afflictions and trials before you can evolve and be the best God has designed you to be.

You must love these daily lessons life and nature dish out for you, my dear, and also ensure to diligently observe and learn well to continue to grow and flourish in all your endeavors.

Day 324

"What makes the world beautiful is how we harness our different abilities to achieve greatness together. No man is an island, and neither are you. We all need each other." – Dr. Sandra C. Duru

Don't Be An Isolated Figure - We All Need Each Other.

There is a place for standing alone and not following the crowd mindlessly regarding ideologies, doctrines, purpose, and plans in life.

However, do you know that, as important as these are, you must also find a way to balance your dealings and interactions with people so that you don't become an isolated person who never reasons or relates well with others?

The Creator made man a social animal; we need one another to grow and progress.

Don't be an isolated figure, my love, because life's beauty combines our unique diversities, ideas, and concepts and builds something amazing together.

Day 325

"Everyone prays to live long. However, the true essence of life is not in the length of years one lives but in the quality of the number of years. Many people go by daily and barely even exist, while others are literally worshipped as gods on this same earth. Which one would you be?" – Dr. Sandra C. Duru

More Than Anything, Quality Trumps Quantity In Life Always.

If you randomly ask about 100 people if they would like to live to a very ripe old age before they pass away, I'm pretty confident that well over 90% of them will surely want to live as long as possible.

Sadly, though, if you are to ask these same set of people how much positive impact they have made in their lives, family, friends, and immediate environment since they were born, many of their answers may make you start wondering why they've even lived to this point at all in the first instance.

Many of us keep going through life, and we're just existing instead of truly living and making something spectacular of our lives. Don't be caught in this web, my dear. More than anything, quality trumps quantity in almost every area of life. Hence, you must always strive to be the best at anything you do and make a positive impact everywhere you find yourself daily.

Day 326

"Stop doubting yourself today because everybody is a genius! All you need to do is find your specific area of gifting and manifest your genius and superb efficiency through it." – Dr. Sandra C. Duru

Nobody Is A Dullard - You Just Have To Find The Right Spark!

My love, at the risk of sounding like a broken record or overkilling this point, I want to remind you today that you are perfectly created and endowed with all you need to thrive and prosper. Hence you should never allow anyone or any circumstances to deceive and tell you otherwise.

An essential duty you owe to yourself in life is to discover who you are and your God-given purpose as early as possible and then fully commit yourself to pursuing such. Nobody was created as a dullard or dead brain, my dear.

You only need to find the right spark and motivation by knowing precisely who you are and what you were created to do, and you will be amazed at the level of extraordinary genius and efficiency you will begin to exude effortlessly!

Day 327

"Life's challenges produce lessons designed to sharpen us and make us better in more ways than one. There's a valuable lesson to learn even in defeat, and you should never miss out on it." – Dr. Sandra C. Duru

Never Waste Any Defeat In Life - You Fell For A Reason.

One of the most exciting things you may probably see and hear today is nature's voice of motivation, reminding you about one vital truth in life - You fall for a reason, and you must find it whenever you do!

No matter what you must battle through and how formidable the obstacles and trials you face, please always remember that nature is not cruel, nor is life against you. They're both programmed to put you through these lessons and phases to bring out the very best version of you.

Hence, you must never waste any lesson you encounter in life, especially your defeats! Ensure you know why and what makes you fall anytime you do, and you will be the best you could ever be in no time when you live that way daily, my love.

Day 328

"No matter how long you live on earth, if you don't do anything to make it impactful, you have not lived a truly fulfilling life." – Dr. Sandra C. Duru

Are You Living Or Simply Existing? Make Your Life Count!

My love, are you aware that there is a thin line between those who are truly alive and others who are merely existing in this world, and you must never be caught on the wrong side of this divide?

It's not about how long you have been on Earth or how many years you eventually live, but the positive and remarkable impact you can make while at it.

Ask yourself this simple question today and answer it as honestly as possible: Are you living or simply existing? How has your time here counted for good and great things in the lives of others around you and beyond, or do you only live for yourself?

That would be such a huge shame, don't you agree? Please start to do better, and make your life count today!

Day 329

> *"Who says you can't start small? Who says you have to wait till you have everything you think you need to set your goals rolling? Begin with the little you have and from wherever you are. You will achieve your goal and even surpass it with dedication and determination."* – Dr. Sandra C. Duru

The Days Of Little Beginnings...Never Underrate Them!

Beloved, have you ever experienced the joy of starting a project from scratch and watching it blossom and flourish until it grows into something remarkable? Oh, this feeling is pretty much indescribable, and it's what nature desires you to experience daily.

Yes, God always desires you to know and experience this joy by building things, dreams, projects, and visions from nothing and seeing them become great. Hence, you must never underrate or despise your days of little and humble beginnings, my dear.

Start with whatever you have right now; stop waiting for a windfall to launch out big. The Creator delights in these steps of faith, and HE will surely bless, increase, and cause you to flourish continually if you follow this voice of nature today!

Day 330

"No matter how hard we try, we cannot escape being hurt by people occasionally. But what's important is how we respond when we find ourselves in such situations. Never become vengeful or bitter." – Dr. Sandra C. Duru

Don't Become Bitter Because Someone Hurt You - Refuse To Be Corrupted!

There is a line from one of the famous music artists renowned for his mega R&B hits that I pondered deeply on the first day I came across it. He said: "Every no-good person was made a no-good by an equally no-good person," and I shook my head sadly.

Don't you see the enemy's vicious cycle and evil plan here, my love? Those who betray, humiliate, attack, and hurt you badly are only weak pawns caught in the enemy's evil web, but you must never allow yourself to be lured into it, too!

Refuse to be corrupted by never becoming bitter and evil, too, whenever someone does you harm or attacks you. Determine that the cycle of hate and bitterness will end with you, my dear, and your life will always be filled with love and victories, no matter what the enemy throws at you.

Day 331

"There is unity and beauty in diversity. Embrace your unique genius and celebrate the diversity in others, too, and your best days are just about to begin in life by so doing." – Dr. Sandra C. Duru

We Are All Uniquely Blessed And Should Embrace One Another, Not Compete.

My love, do you know that even if one trillion birds were to take flight simultaneously, there would be more than enough space for each one to spread its wings and soar to any heights it wants to in the heavens?

Nature is designed to accommodate everyone with our unique individualities and special talents, and we're supposed to coexist peacefully, not jealously attack and drag each other down.

Learn to tap into the unlimited human resources and skills around you and embrace the uniqueness of others, too, my dear. You will be glad as the results of this wisdom begin to unfold in all that concerns you continually from today.

Day 332

> *"If you decide to wait till you have everything figured out, you may have to wait for long, and if not careful, forever. Nobody is ever ready, and there is never a perfect time to do anything in this life."* – Dr. Sandra C. Duru

Waiting To Start When You're Ready Is Waiting To Never Start - Don't Play Yourself!

If you are one of those who always want to see the clouds gathering before they go out to cultivate their land and plant their seeds, this voice of nature and life is for you today.

Those who wait for the perfect time to get started on their dreams, visions, goals, and God-given purpose almost always end up never achieving anything meaningful with their skill, time, and immense gifts because there is never a perfect time for anything!

My love, waiting to start when you feel you're ready and everything is right is equivalent to waiting never to start. Don't play yourself for a fool, my dear. Get to it today!

Day 333

"Life will not always present us with what we ask of it. It is left to us to make do with whatever we have at our disposal. There is no shame in starting small. The real shame is not starting at all." – Dr. Sandra C. Duru

The Best Is Not Who Started Big, But Who Started At All!

My love, what is that dream, goal, and vision that you have been nursing and trying to get started but haven't made a move because you're afraid of being mocked because you have no great resources to launch out with presently?

Don't allow the enemy to rob you of the greatness and limitless blessings God has gifted you with by tricking you into focusing on what you don't have today instead of what you will potentially have if you make that move right now.

The best in life are not those who got to start big, my dear, but those who got to start at all! No matter how little or insignificant you have in your hands, place them before your Maker, ask for HIS blessings, and launch out today! You will be glad you did in the long run.

Voice Of Nature (Vol.1) By Sandra Duru

Day 334

"There is always a lesson to be learned whether we win or lose. The only time it would be a loss is when the person has not identified the reason for the loss and learned from it so that such won't repeat itself anymore." – Dr. Sandra C. Duru

You Only Lose When You Don't Learn...Not When You Fall.

The wise say that failure is not final because no matter how hard you fall, you have not been defeated until you refuse to get back up again. Hence, my love, you must understand today that you can never lose unless you choose to!

How do you choose to lose? Refusing to learn from your mistakes and turning that knowledge and experience into the wisdom you need to overcome that obstacle whenever it rises against you again. That's when you choose to lose, my dear.

You only lose when you refuse to learn from your mistakes, shortcomings, and even victories, not when you fall or supposedly fail. Know this, and know peace today, my love.

Day 335

> *"There is never a permanent friend or foe in this life, and the sooner you have and efficiently use this piece of wisdom, the better for you, my dear."* – Dr. Sandra C. Duru

A Foe Today Can Be A Friend Tomorrow - Never Burn Bridges!

My love, as much as you are tasked with always being on guard against evil and despicable people masquerading as friends around you, do you know that you must do this wisely because nothing lasts forever?

Yes, this includes friendship and enmity, too, my dear. Hence, you must be careful not to destroy some bridges because of today's unpleasant encounters, as you may never know if you will need those same bridges tomorrow.

A foe and enemy today can become a friend tomorrow due to prevailing circumstances and needs, so you must always walk in wisdom with all men!

Day 336

"We need to understand when to hold on and when to walk away from something not working in our favor. Never keep yourself in a toxic environment." – Dr. Sandra C. Duru

Toxic People And Environments Will Drown You - Walk Away!

My beloved friend, there is a point in your life where you must understand that nothing else can help or save you but the wisdom that comes from abiding with your Maker's wisdom, which is all around you in nature. And what does this wisdom say today?

Learn how to balance and sift through everything in and around your life - people, businesses, information, relationships, and everything else. Toxic people, things, situations, and environments will not only drain you, but they will drown and snuff life out of you, too!

Hence, you must never hesitate to cut off entirely and distance yourself from such, my dear. You shouldn't burn bridges entirely, but never encourage, condone, or permit toxicity around you.

Day 337

"Whatever you do in life, make sure you're moving forward. It doesn't matter how fast or slow you move. Just ensure you are progressing and getting better at whatever you set out to do." – Dr. Sandra C. Duru

Seek Improvement, Not Speed Daily - It's How Well, Not How Fast!

Are you aware that life does not care about who gets things done first or fastest but who can get them done and sustain them as well?

Hence, my love, your priority must never be about how fast you can accomplish something but how you can sustain it after getting it done! This is one of the reasons why wealth hardly transits from generation to many generations down the line - people are in such a hurry they don't bother to build to last!

It is how well, and not how fast, you can get to your purpose and dreams in life, my dear. Hence, you must always seek improvement and mastery over speed daily.

Day 338

"If we were not supposed to be social creatures, HE would not have put the need to co-exist and intermingle inside us. Hence, you must learn to sit back, keep quiet, and listen to others around you, too, from time to time.." – Dr. Sandra C. Duru

No Man Is An Island - Listen To Others Too!

My love, do you know that a person's downfall irrevocably begins when they conclude that they know it all and never need advice or anyone's assistance?

Even the greatest generals and captains always need equally able lieutenants because nobody can ever know it all!

No man is an island, my dear, so you must learn to listen to others and always glean from their knowledge, experience, and wisdom. Only the Almighty God is all-knowing and sufficient all by Himself. You are not God, are you?

Day 339

"You can't continue to live another person's dream. You must fashion out your life to be a reference point for people to follow." – Dr. Sandra C. Duru

Stop Living Another Person's Life - What Is Your Purpose On Earth?

My dear friend, there comes a time when you must consider several things and thoroughly audit your life and how you've been living it because you owe that much to yourself to do right by yourself.

I agree that loyalty and selflessness are great virtues everyone should have. However, you must never be so selfless that you now fail to have a life, purpose, vision, and dreams, as this is total folly and nothing virtuous!

Stop living other people's lives and dreams at the detriment of yours. What is your purpose on earth, and how far have you established it yet? Think about this call from nature today, my love, and hopefully, you will set yourself on the right path if you have been walking wrongly before.

Day 340

"It is virtually impossible to avoid getting talked about and criticized by people in this life because they must always have something to say no matter what you do or do not do. Pay them no attention, and stay focused." – Dr. Sandra C. Duru

People Will Always Talk - Don't Be Discouraged By That!

Do you know that one of the most impossible things to experience in this world is to go through life without having people talk about you one way or another? Tongues are created to wag, my love, so why should they ever deter you?

You need to build your mental toughness to the point where every side talk - either positive or negative - rolls off you like water rolls off a rock without ever penetrating it. People will always talk, my dear, so you must never be discouraged or pulled down by whatever anyone says about you!

It's their mouth, but it's your life; hence, you should never give anyone such power over you.

Day 341

"Leave the past where it belongs. Let bygones be bygones. A new chapter is open for you. Embrace it today!" – Dr. Sandra C. Duru

Never Bring Yesterday's Troubles Into Today - Leave Old Things Be!

The words of the Master concerning putting new wine into old wineskins readily come to mind as nature's voice comes this morning, my love. Even Jesus admits it will be a colossal waste as the skin will burst and waste the wine!

This happens whenever you refuse to leave the past where it is and keep dragging old, dead, and gone issues into every new day of your life. Stop robbing and shortchanging yourself this way, my dear!

Leave old issues, pain, hurts, and things where they are, and never bring yesterday's troubles into your today. Why rob yourself of the peace nature and your Creator desire for you by refusing to let go?

Day 342

"There's more to life than you being the center of attention all the time. Have you ever tried listening to people in the hope that they would talk, instead of always talking & hoping that people will listen?"
— Dr. Sandra

Learn To Sit Back And Learn, Too, Sometimes - The World Doesn't Revolve Around You!

My love, are you aware that refusing to allow anyone else to talk or do things around you will eventually lead to you burning out and exhausting yourself before your time?

God gave everyone HE created a brain and reasoning abilities and then put us all together on earth so that we may help ourselves occasionally and relieve each other's burdens.

Learn to sit back, relax, unwind, and learn from others, too, my dear. The world does not revolve around you; hence, you cannot always be the go-to person! Why should you extinguish your flames and die before your time by doing too much, my dear?

Day 343

"Don't ever follow the crowd, but let the crowd be the one to follow after you instead. It's as simple as it sounds. Never be the one to adjust to the dictates of the crowd; instead, be the one that calls the shots." – Dr. Sandra C. Duru

Do You Have Personal Convictions, Or You're A Crowd Pleaser?

This is a question that nature puts to everyone today, as this sort of self-evaluation and assessment is vital to your growth, longevity, and overall well-being, my love.

Do you have personal convictions, policies, and beliefs that you value, follow, and hold dear, or are you blown about by whatever is trending online or whatever everyone else says to you?

You are so much more and better than such a life, my dear, and you need to quit being a crowd-pleaser from today if that's how you live! God did not make you become a toy in anyone else's hands, no matter who they are!

So, you must invest in finding your God-given purpose and immersing yourself fully in it because a life of purpose and vision can never be tossed around and follow the crowd like that. You were created to be royalty and an impactful soul, my dear. Please start living like one!

Day 344

"You need to look around you for greater and better opportunities rather than dissipate energy trying to resurrect a dead cause. Learn from it and move on because if you dwell too much on it, you may get carried away and end up missing out on the fresh opportunity that the disappointment birthed." – Dr. Sandra C. Duru

Go After New Opportunities - Stop Wailing Over Spilt Milk!

Are you aware that one of the most dangerous and saddest ways you shortchange and rob yourself is when you refuse to move on from dead things and look out for new and better ones, my love?

It could be a failed relationship, business, marriage, project, or anything you're desperately hanging on to, even though you know it's dead and gone. You're not doing yourself any favors or good at all, my dear, and you must desist from such harmful behavior.

Learn from whatever mistakes you made, mourn your loss for a little while, and by all means, please move on and go after new opportunities instead of sitting there and crying over your already spilled milk! Nothing good will ever come out of that, so stop wasting your time and life on such, please.

Voice Of Nature (Vol.1) By Sandra Duru

Day 345

"Nobody has the monopoly of knowledge. Give other people a chance to express themselves. It will amaze you how much you can learn from them when you calmly listen to others around you." – Dr. Sandra C. Duru

A Calm Man Is A Wise Man - Your Learning And Growth Is Boundless!

Have you ever been told that one of the fastest and best ways to evolve and become better is by learning and gleaning from others around you and applying all you've learned in your personal life and journey daily?

No, you don't have to know and do everything to be the best, my love. There's no shame in admitting that you're not all-knowing and allowing others to teach and guide you on some things you need, too, no matter how little.

Life works best for all when we all have a shoulder to lean on and some extra heads of wisdom to glean from, my dear. Don't deprive yourself of this joy and comfort for any reason.

Day 346

"You must never look like the opposite of what you're trying to make people see or believe! Always do your best to look the part; it would be easier to sell your dreams, ideas, and vision to others." – Dr.Sandra C. Duru

People Buy What They See Before Anything Else - Don't Be Fake.

You often see a product in a package or container and feel it would be great because of how it looks there, only for you to get up close even to buy it and have instant regrets. If you can relate to this, then this note from nature is for you today, my love.

No matter the urge to make yourself "attractive or sellable," never present yourself as something you know you're not to anyone else. Once trust and integrity are eroded, they can never be regained, and you can never tell where such a silly error will haunt you terribly in the future.

Don't ever be fake because people buy what they see before the actual product itself. Avoid making a little profit today that will cost you your career tomorrow!

Day 347

"All is vanity on this earth; hence, we must always seek understanding as we navigate our daily pursuits, and we will excel." – Dr. Sandra C. Duru

Never Put Your Trust In Earthly Things - All Is Vanity!

My love, do you know that the most important thing you must acquire as you go about your daily hustle and pursue your dreams and purpose is a perfect understanding of how nature and everything around you work?

Nothing is ever as it appears in life; hence, you must gain profound understanding and never take anything at face value, my love! All is vanity, and nothing lasts forever, so you must never put your trust and hope in anything else but God in this world.

This understanding will help you navigate the tricky and rocky paths of life, and you, too, will achieve your purpose in life sooner than later if you remain steadfast in it.

Day 348

"There is a way that you should go as you seek to achieve your set goals and objectives, and this is the way of wisdom. Those who walk in this way are highly regarded by others and always celebrated as being exceptional in all things." – Dr. Sandra C. Duru

Wisdom Is The Only Path You Should Seek And Follow - It's The Way Of Life!

The best and most vital thing that can happen to anyone preparing to embark on a journey is knowing the exact routes needed, how they should navigate them, and when to pass through each one. Such trips are often so smooth and enjoyable that you want to repeat them repeatedly.

This is what wisdom offers to those who have it, my love, and why you must covet it above everything else. Knowing how to go about your tasks as you pursue your purpose in life already eliminates more than half of the stress you could face.

Hence, you must seek wisdom, find it, and never cease to walk in its paths, for in it is life, glory, honor, success, and every good thing you could ever desire. Yes, wisdom is life itself, and you will do well to find it!

Day 349

"That you failed while on the verge of hitting your goal does not mean it's the end. When you fail, you must try and keep trying again. Persistence is vital in achieving our goals in life." – Dr. Sandra C. Duru

Winners Are Persistent Beings - Failure Is Never Final For Them.

Are you aware that the only difference between a renowned champion and others in any field is the determination, persistence, and relentless zeal always to hit the mark and never be average?

That's the defining factor, my love, and you must develop this same mentality to break through every obstacle before you and get to your desired goals. Failure is never an outcome for winners because they're persistent and will never take no for an answer.

Never let a temporary setback like your shortcomings, mistakes, or failures end your quest for greatness, my dear. Keep pressing on!

Day 350

"You must engage your imaginations and your mind a bit more, too, and you will be amazed at the endless possibilities and greatness you can achieve!" – Dr. Sandra C. Duru

You Carry Way More Than You're Utilizing Yet - Put Yourself To Good Use!

My love, I know the voice of nature has called our attention to some lessons we can enjoy from the story of little David and the mighty Goliath, but there is one question still to ask you today.

Do you know what separated David from every other man and soldier in Israel on that fateful day? It was his knowledge of the power he had behind and within himself, and more importantly, his willingness to tap into and use it to the fullest, too. The result of that willingness and confidence was a victory for the people of God and a name we still refer to, celebrate, and talk about to date.

Like David, are you aware that you carry more than you presently utilize or even acknowledge? You are not of them that should ever be put to flight by any obstacle, tribulation, or trial because the greatest one in all of the creation dwells in you!

My dear, put yourself to good use because your possibilities are limitless.

Day 351

"Be extra and intentional about life. Develop the capacity to inspire others with your mindset and skill set. Don't be the type of person who expects people to do what you cannot do in the name of being their leader." – Dr. Sandra C. Duru

If You Want Something Done, Do It Yourself First - Be A Great Leader Always.

If there is one quality any leader can possess that would inspire his followers to go through anything life throws at them without flinching, it is the wisdom and humility to never ask for something they can't or haven't already done themselves!

Such is the way of a truly great leader, my love, and you are created, called, equipped, and ordained to be precisely this and even much more. Never ask or expect people to do what you cannot do yourself. It demeans and rubbished your authority as a leader.

Hence, you must be deliberate about how you live and lead others around you. You are the first example for them in many ways, so please set the right ones.

Day 352

"Nothing can market a great product more than the product itself, and you do not need to sweat or struggle to force people over. Quality can draw people closer than your words of persuasion or eloquence ever will." – Dr. Sandra C. Duru

Quality Speaks Louder Than Words - Put In Your All Always!

If truth be told, my love, I must confess that I have always found it fascinating how water and some other food items never get advertised anywhere, yet almost nothing sells out faster than them.

However, I've discovered over the years that because of the quality and extreme value these items represent and provide, they are and will continue to be among the most sought-after things on this planet. Hence, nature's voice to you today.

You don't need to spend resources on advertising or marketing if you completely pour yourself into your plans, dreams, goals, and projects. A great product markets and sells itself, my dear, because quality speaks louder than words.

So you must never hold back whenever you're preparing and doing things related to your life and purpose, and you will enjoy this level of ease and acceptability, too.

Day 353

"Life is full of lots of challenges, but what we make of it determines whether we're victims of the circumstance we are faced with or not." – Dr. Sandra C. Duru

Challenges Will Always Be There. What Will You Do About Them?

Of so many things that life is always known to harbor and hold for all, challenges, trials, tribulations, and obstacles are constants that will never cease to be, my love. Hence, the question now is, what will you do about them?

Are you going to face them head-on and never retreat or surrender till you surmount and conquer them all, or do you want to coil up in a corner and continue wailing like a helpless victim? The choice is all yours, my dear.

Life will continually treat you the way you permit and always allow it to treat you, so you must refuse to be trampled and subdued because the Creator didn't make you the vanquished but the victor!

Day 354

"Greatness is not cheap. It comes with sacrifice, and your temptation for greatness will fuel the drive to be able to sacrifice so much. Many successful and great people widely regard this temptation as the 'biggest drug in the world.'" – Dr. Sandra C. Duru

How Tempted Are You For Success? How Badly Do You Want It?

My love, do you know that no matter how much we talk about being great, accomplished, successful, and fulfilled, some people are never bothered and would never move a muscle to reach such heights in life?

Yes, there are many whose most significant goal is only to have at least one meal in a day and a roof over their head, no matter how it looks or where it is. You cannot blame anyone for not having ambitions to better their lives if they don't want to.

Such people know there is a steep price to pay to rise above the mediocrity and penury their lives are steeped in but are unwilling to pay it. So to you today, this call from nature asks: What are you willing to do to succeed, be legitimately prosperous in life, and fulfill your God-given purpose, my dear?

Nothing is impossible for those who believe and are determined to achieve them, but how badly do you genuinely want that success and greatness?

Day 355

"What's your current situation like? What are you going to do about it? Will you let that situation weigh you down and make you a victim? Don't do that. Rise and soar above it like the champion you are!" – Dr. Sandra C. Duru

What Do You Do When Affliction And Troubles Come Knocking?

My beloved friend, are you aware that some things need to be said only once, while others require a great degree of consistent repetition before they can break into the minds of those they're directed at? Faith does come by hearing the right words repeatedly, remember?

Nature's voice has stated this repeatedly over the years. Still, it doesn't hurt to remind you as many times as possible again, my love: You are a born champion, and no circumstance or situation can ever subvert or change that!

So, my dear, keep this truth in mind whatever you're battling and struggling against today. It is only a matter of time before your salvation, and victory shall manifest before all, so never succumb to the pressures your situation is mounting upon you. You are not a victim!

Day 356

"You must never be afraid or hesitant to use the word "No" whenever the need arises so that you can maintain a strict order or balance and clarity around you always." – Dr. Sandra C. Duru

Your Sanity Is Your Responsibility - Never Hesitate To Say No When Needed!

As a loving and caring mother, I hardly hold back any affection from my children and always do my best to give them anything they need to make their lives comfortable, productive, and purposeful.

However, my love, I also do not hesitate to say no to them on numerous occasions whenever I notice them crossing the line. Do you know you must adopt this same strategy when dealing with others in and around your space?

People will continually treat you how you allow them to, so you must draw the line for where your tolerance and love expire, and never be afraid or hesitant to put your foot down as you say a firm "NO!" to their excesses. In the long run, my dear, it is for your own good.

Day 357

"Your work can speak, and when it does, you just have to enjoy the view because you put in the much-needed effort. When your work speaks for itself, by its extraordinary quality and uniqueness, you must keep quiet and let it do the talking." – Dr. Sandra C. Duru

Learn To Relax And Enjoy The Fruits Of Your Labor - YOLO Indeed, Remember?

My darling, if there's ever a time when the acronym "Y.O.L.O" makes perfect sense, it is whenever it comes to you getting to lean back and enjoy the fruits of your labor from time to time!

You only live once, so you must learn to enjoy yourself and take some much-needed breaks from working hard and doing everything yourself.

When you have given your all to your purpose, vision, and projects, and they start to shine and speak excellently, don't try to do anything other than relax and milk the attention and momentum they give you to the fullest! You deserve it, my love, so please enjoy them now.

Voice Of Nature (Vol.1) By Sandra Duru

Day 358

"A good relationship with others creates a happier, healthier environment, boosting overall productivity and performance. How do you relate with others around you?" – Dr. Sandra C. Duru

Bad Energy Drains Everyone Without Exception - Keep Things Cordial Always.

Do you know that any times when you sue for peace and tranquility around you, it's not because you're weak or afraid of conflicts but because you are a wise student of nature, my love?

Yes, wisdom will let you know that bad and negative energy drains everyone wherever they exist without exception; hence, you would do well to keep things smooth, peaceful, and cordial with everyone around you as much as you can.

Always be mindful of how you relate with others in your space, as this creates the atmosphere that will be prevalent around you, and you don't want to battle and deal with such negativity constantly, do you?

Day 359

"As a leader, you must live up to the standard you set and even beyond. Don't ask people to do something you are unwilling to do yourself. Once those around you know that you always lead by example, it becomes effortless for them to follow you and give their all." – Dr. Sandra C. Duru

When You Give All, You Will Get All - It Starts With You!

Many times in life, we ascribe the act of leading by example to only those in the limelight, but do you know that this is precisely how every one of us is supposed to live daily, my beloved?

The motivation and inspiration you're trying too hard to give your children, spouse, siblings, friends, and others should begin from and with you. By giving your all in everything you do before them, you naturally motivate them to do the same when it comes to you.

Hence, it is true that when you give your all in life, you're bound to receive all in return, too, and you have the right to expel anything that gives you less! However, please ensure that you have always led by example and set the proper standards before making demands of anyone around you. That is only when it is fair with nature and the Creator.

Day 360

"You must protect and invest in your mind because even the greatest ideas can be aborted when the mind is saturated with the wrong information. Never allow fear to creep in." – Dr. Sandra C. Duru

A Corrupted Mind Can Abort Anything - Keep Yours Sanitized Always!

In one of HIS numerous parables while on earth, the Master told of a farmer who had planted good seeds on his farm and went to bed, but when they grew, they were filled with numerous nasty weeds. Have you ever pondered on how HE explained this parable, my love?

Jesus said that the farm is your heart, the good seeds are the lofty ideas, dreams, and visions you have, but the weeds are the doubts, fears, and evil thoughts the enemy sneaks in and plants into your mind while you're unguarded.

A corrupt mind can abort even the brightest ideas and destroy the best projects, so you must guard yours diligently and continually sanitize and weed through it daily!

Keep your mind free of fear, doubt, and unbelief, and your success is as sure as the sun rising and setting daily, my dear.

Day 361

"Our imaginations are much more potent than we think or know they are, and we need to engage them more than we currently do. Every invention – good or bad – we see today started from imagination." – Dr. Sandra C. Duru

This World Was Created By Imagination - How Do You Use Yours?

"And God said, Let there be light..." and the rest is history, as we fondly say, yet this holds a vital lesson from nature for everyone today. The story of creation tells of how the Creator called things that did not exist forth, and immediately, they all came to be.

Now, where did HE call them forth, and how did HE see them before doing so? In HIS mind and with the power of imagination, for sure! Guess what, my love? You were given that same power and ability when HE created you, and then he commissioned you to rule, dominate, and subdue the earth in HIS stead!

Everything you see and know today was conceived and created through the power of imagination. How do you use yours today, my dear? It is not mere motivational or inspirational cliches whenever I tell you that you are more powerful than you think and are unstoppable. It is the undiluted truth!

Day 362

> *"Do you know that you are not here in this world to only survive day to day, earn your living, probably raise a family, and just grow old and pass away? No, you are created for more than these mundane things!"*
> – Dr. Sandra C. Duru

You Are Created To Thrive, Not To Merely Exist!

My love, how would you feel if you ever saw someone buy a Mercedes SLK 500, cut off the entire roof, smash the side doors so they don't open anymore, and start using it to transport thrash around your city? Did I feel your mind almost go wild just trying to picture such a sacrilege?

Well, what if I told you that this is precisely how you make God feel every time HE sees you barely even surviving after HE created you to rule, dominate, and excel in life? You were created and born to thrive in life, my dear; hence, your existence should mean so much more than just earning a living and getting your daily bread.

You are destined for more extraordinary things, so you must strive to do more and be more from today, my dear.

Day 363

"Never be afraid of being wrong. Why? You get to learn, become stronger and tougher, and you also get to start seeing things from a different perspective. The worst thing to do is nothing." – Dr. Sandra C. Duru

Doing Nothing Is Worse Than Making Mistakes - Choose Wisely!

Are you aware that there is and will always be a massive difference between a person who makes mistakes even repeatedly and someone who does nothing at all?

One may be called a fool, but the truth is that they're growing and making progress steadily, no matter how tiny! The other one who refuses to do anything for fear of making mistakes, though, will not only never gain anything or improve in any way, but there's also the possibility of retrogressing because you're either going forward or backward in life. There is no middle ground!

This is why doing nothing is far worse than making mistakes, my love. At least, you will be making progress no matter how tiny when you continue making attempts to get better, so what have you got to lose?

Day 364

"There is a massive power in the mind and our thoughts. Your mind is the invisible starting point for any tangible achievement. The world's best inventions today started with a thought. Use yours well, too!" – Dr.Sandra C. Duru

What Have You Created With The Power Of Your Mind? Stop Wasting It!

No matter how we look at and judge some people, they have put their minds to use in the best possible ways they felt they could, and their impacts - good or evil - are still felt today. The question and simple voice nature brings to you right now is, what have you done with yours since you were born, my dear?

Left untapped, the mind's powers will remain dormant and continue wasting away, and it is such a vast, sad shame considering how incredibly potent and limitless it is!

Everything you are praying for and desire is at your fingertips already, my love, and you can surely grab and actualize them if only you would put this incredible power within you to good use. Please stop wasting yours.

Day 365

"Don't settle for a life void of impact and usefulness to others. Never hesitate to do more and be more because you're made for so much more." – Dr. Sandra C. Duru

You Are Called To Be More And Do More - Nothing Else Is Acceptable!

What at the most significant obstacles and challenges you've ever faced from birth to date, my love, and how are you dealing with them now?

What if I told you that the worst things you've ever experienced are nothing but a tiny breath compared to the glory God has created and destined you for? Oh, yes, my dear, they are nothing compared to all you will become once you achieve your purpose and maximize your full potential!

So, knowing this, why would you ever choose to settle for a life of mediocrity and zero impact? Why would you choose to be an enslaved person in a palace where you've been crowned king?

You were created and born to be more and do more in life, my dear. Anything less than this is entirely unacceptable to nature and your Creator, so please sit up and live right from today!

CONCLUSION | YEAR-END AUDIT:

As with many other years that we've had the grace and privilege to see to an end, this one has come and gone, too.

However, specific questions linger and should be adequately treated and settled before you plunge into another year before you. A wise man once said that insanity is doing the same thing the same way repeatedly while expecting a different outcome.

This book was designed to be as instructional as it is inspirational and motivational. Hence, the crux of its focus is how well you've improved your life while documenting every minute of it throughout the year.

How well have you been able to hear and adapt to the voice of nature all around you, and how well did it also impact your life and daily chronicles all year?

If you want to gauge how efficiently well you lived through the year, take this year-end audit below and answer the questions as truthfully and clearly as possible.

Remember: It's your life, and you have the power to make of it whatever you desire and will. And, as long as you diligently follow after wisdom - especially through resource materials such as this book - it can and will only get better every passing day for the rest of your life. Amen!

YEAR-END AUDIT:

(1) What were your constraints, challenges, and most difficult obstacles during the year?

(2) How were you able to overcome them?

(3) What would you do differently this year If you could turn back the hands of time?

(4) What new things did you discover about yourself this year?

(5) How do you intend to harness, develop, and eventually create value from these things (if any) going forward?

NOTES

NOTES

SYNOPSIS

Popular Nigerian-born African-American Business Magnate, Humanitarian, and Media & PR Expert Dr. Sandra Chidinma Duru has published motivational and inspirational quotes, articles, and journals across several media platforms daily for over 22 years on her websites: www.mgbeke.media and www.wenetly.com.

And, if anyone knows how it feels to be written off and cast aside as a no-good, it is Dr. Duru. Hence, she has dedicated her life to nurturing, motivating, inspiring, mentoring, and helping those who have also been written off to do more and be more in life.

This book offers daily motivational and wisdom nuggets designed to inspire and provoke readers to be more direct and intentional about their daily lives.

While helping them develop mental toughness as they apply the daily nuggets, it is also designed to help any seemingly average person with no recognized writing skills develop a passion for it by documenting their daily activities while also grooming several top writers among them, too, in the process.

Dr. Duru is also a renowned Information Strategist, Talent Acquisition Manager, street-smart spiritual warrior, and a self-taught, highly-driven, and highly motivated individual whose life story and personal experiences are touching and deeply inspirational.

She is also the author of the best-selling motivational and inspirational book, "Soul Tonic - A Daily Motivational & Inspirational Guide (Vol.1)."

www.ingramcontent.com/pod-product-compliance
Lightning Source LLC
Chambersburg PA
CBHW010247010526
44119CB00007B/184